Developing Early Childhood Services

Developing Early Childhood Services

Past, Present and Future

Peter Baldock

 Open University Press

Open University Press
McGraw-Hill Education
McGraw-Hill House
Shoppenhangers Road
Maidenhead
Berkshire
England
SL6 2QL

email: enquiries@openup.co.uk
world wide web: www.openup.co.uk

and Two Penn Plaza, New York, NY 10121-2289, USA

First published 2011

A catalogue record of this book is available from the British Library

ISBN-13: 978-0-33-523873-6 (pb) 978-0-33-523874-3 (hb)
ISBN-10: 0-33-523873-4 (pb) 0-33-523874-2 (hb)
eISBN: 978-0-33-523875-0

Library of Congress Cataloging-in-Publication Data
CIP data applied for

Typeset by RefineCatch Limited, Bungay, Suffolk
Printed in the UK by Bell and Bain Ltd, Glasgow

Fictitious names of companies, products, people, characters and/or data that may
be used herein (in case studies or in examples) are not intended to represent any
real individual, company, product or event.

Mixed Sources

Product group from well-managed
forests and other controlled sources
www.fsc.org   Cert no. TT-COC-002769
© 1996 Forest Stewardship Council

FSC

The *McGraw-Hill* Companies

Contents

Acknowledgements

I would like to put on record my thanks to all of those who gave me generous assistance in the writing of this book.

I was helped with access to archive material or histories of their organizations by Neil Hart (London Early Years Foundation), Nicola Hilliard (National Children's Bureau), Letitia Lawson (Bradford Central Library Archives), Rebecca Loader (National Childminding Association), Kate Neil (Pre-school Learning Alliance), Severine Njock (Day Care Trust), Liz Roberts (*Nursery World*), Nina Smith (Council for Awards in Children's Care and Education), Loreen Williams (4Children) and Hayley Wilson (National Day Nurseries Association).

I wish to thank people for their kind permission to include quotations from the following: Adrian Harris for material first appearing on the *Blue Blog*; Ed Balls for the quotation from his personal blog; Liz Roberts for material first published in *Nursery World*; Taylor & Francis for the extract from Bertha, Baroness von Marenholtz-Bülow's book *Woman's Educational Mission* in the translation by Elizabeth, Countess Krockow von Wickerode, reprinted in K.J. Brehony (ed.) *Mother's Songs and Selected Writings* published by Routledge in 2001; and Wales PPA for the extract from their 2008 publication *Memories of the Playgroup Movement in Wales 1961–1987*.

I also want to thank members of staff at Adsetts Centre (Sheffield Hallam University); Joule Library (University of Manchester); Manchester Central Library (Local History and Archives); Sheffield Central Library (Reference and Local History Sections); and Western Bank Library (University of Sheffield).

Several friends and colleagues helped me with ideas and information on particular topics, including Perry Else, David Lane, Rosemary Lilley, Peter McBride, Linda McMahon, Sue Owen, Sheila Shinman and Valerie Wood.

I also want to thank Judy Michie, Sue Owen and Caroline Poland who read earlier drafts of this book and helped me with critical comment. I remain, of course, responsible for the book itself.

Introduction

Why write about the history of early childhood services?

This book describes the development of our early childhood services. In the terms we use today it is about the origins and expansion of day nurseries, nursery education, playwork and support services for parents of young children.

You may want to ask why anyone should bother with the past; whether it is not the present and the future that matter. I hope the answer to that will emerge as the book progresses, but I will attempt an initial response now because the question is a good one. As far as I know, this is the first attempt to describe the development of such services as a whole, although there is some admirable material on specific topics. The subject does not have the profile it might have. You could compile a quite respectable list of authoritative books covering between them the social history of our country over the last five hundred years and find the care and education of the youngest children rarely mentioned, if mentioned at all. Similarly, authors of books on early childhood services often have little to say about the historical background. There are exceptions, such as Bilton (1998) and Penn (2005), but they are comparatively rare.

There are factors that help explain, without justifying, this neglect. The care and education of children have usually been seen as the responsibility of mothers, and anything done by women who were not monarchs or other public figures failed until fairly recently to attract the interest of historians.

The fact that none of us have very clear episodic memories of our earliest years (the phenomenon known as 'infantile amnesia') has prevented memories of those years from finding their way into the records. Certainly, the growing literature on the history of childhood has more to say about children over 7 years of age than it does about those who were younger than that.

The reasons for neglecting the subject may be unjustified, but a more positive case has to be made for seeing the history of early childhood services as worth attention. There are two important reasons for studying our history. First, the story of early childhood services helps to illustrate in a particularly graphic manner the ways in which the relationships between adults and children, families and their communities, society and government have been changing over a long period of time. It is an aspect of our social history deserving more attention. Second, a study of history can illuminate the present situation of those services and assist us in understanding recent developments and what might happen next.

The background: urbanization and its impact

In the less technologically developed communities of the past, little was said about the particular needs of children. This does not mean that no importance was attached to them or that there was any lack of affection. However, in such societies everyone had to contribute to production if everyone was to survive. It was obvious that very young children would be able to offer a smaller contribution because of their limited experience and strength. It was also clear that babies needed particular care (as did some adults). Nevertheless, for the most part, children joined the adult world in work and in play. A few particularly perceptive individuals appreciated how children were able to create a world of their own. For the most part the idea of a separate world of childhood that might require particular understanding barely emerged over many centuries.

That development began as we moved to a predominantly urban form of social organization. Great cities have existed for a long time – 'great' in the sense that they were large, had impressive achievements and dominated their surrounding areas. A fully urban society only began to emerge in Europe in modern times and it did so first in England. Urbanization was closely associated with the Industrial Revolution of the eighteenth and nineteenth centuries. That phenomenon was based to some extent on workforce organization required for the intensive production of warships for the Royal Navy. It was accelerated by technical invention. The reorganization of agriculture was yet another driver of urbanization. England changed during the sixteenth, seventeenth and eighteenth centuries from what had been a largely subsistence economy to one where different regions of the country specialized in the kind of foodstuff or other agricultural goods, such as leather, they produced. Trade, as opposed to the meeting of very local needs, had a growing place in agricultural production. Estates became more extensive and were more efficiently managed. The rural economy needed fewer labourers. This drove many people into the towns that became major cities and created the possibility of mass production and consumption, a process that had started in London as early as the sixteenth century.

The change to an urbanized and industrialized society in the nineteenth century was rapid. By the 1840s the urban population of England was twice the size of the rural one. By the end of the nineteenth century the majority of the population of the whole United Kingdom lived in towns and cities rather than the countryside or small towns.

The transformation was large in scale and was felt as a sudden change, but aspects of an older society survived for some time. My grandmother was woken on her first morning in her marital home by the sound of sheep being driven to graze in fields nearby – in Camden Town in the middle of London. Further back in time the first factories were not the highly organized single units of production they later became, but collections of workshops gathered in particular places to make it easier to bring in raw materials, use water-power and transport finished goods to where they were wanted. There was considerable continuity between the older system where production was mainly conducted in the family home or on the family land and the industrialized system. A long time passed before the stricter separation of work and home developed.

The attempt to understand the new urban society and what its needs might be (including the needs of its young children) only got off the ground once that society was well established. Feelings and spontaneous reactions came before analysis. There were those, especially in the first half of the nineteenth century, who regarded the phenomenon with fear. It was common for politicians and journalists to compare the new urban working class to the barbarian hordes who had overwhelmed ancient Rome. To some extent, fear was counterbalanced by the pride of those who created the new industrial cities, a pride expressed in the construction of ornate town halls. Sociological analysis of the urban phenomenon came later than fear or pride in achievement. Even then, for many, the urban masses remained strange and potentially frightening. Talk of an ominous underclass emerged at frequent intervals. As late as the 1960s sociologists were describing working-class communities in ways remarkably similar to those employed by social anthropologists to describe societies in the remotest parts of the southern hemisphere. Frankenberg (1966) offers a summary of several of these studies.

If many aspects of the older economy survived into the twentieth century, it was also true that the transformation of British and especially English society started before the Industrial Revolution was well underway. It had already been apparent in the sixteenth century, which felt the impact of the disintegration of the old aristocracy by the Wars of the Roses, the break-up of the Catholic Church with the Reformation and the discovery of new worlds and the opportunities they offered for trade and self-enrichment. It is for this reason that the next chapter starts with the Tudors rather than two or three hundred years later.

The unfinished story

The history of early childhood services is far from being complete yet. It is not only that more needs to be done to make them more effective. The factors that have complicated and impeded the growth of those services in the past are still with us. As a society we have not yet got to grips fully with the consequences of the massive change in social life that large-scale urbanization has produced and we have not done so mainly because the process is nowhere near an end. An understanding of history is important to how we tackle things today because it is about more than the past. The present itself is part of history.

An introductory essay

This account of how early childhood services reached the situation they were in at the time of the general election of 2010 is only an initial, exploratory essay. I have been unable to write as much on many topics as I would have wished.

As there is already a good deal of material on the pioneers of thinking about early education, I have said less on their theories than I might have done and focused on organizational growth and policy.

This is principally an account of what happened in England. There are references to Scotland, Wales and Ireland (especially when they had an impact on England) but limited space has not allowed me to describe the achievements of those countries in the detail that they warrant. I regret this all the more because descriptions of what happened in the parts of the UK outside England have often been distorted by conflicting views on national identity. To take just one example, David Stow, the founder of the Glasgow Infant School Society in 1827, has been praised in his own country as an example of their superiority in education, while English writers, such as Rusk (1933: 158–64) have often dismissed him as a nice enough chap, but only an imitator of what he had learned from London.

My principal regret is that I have been unable to say more than I have about many lesser-known personalities. Some individuals, such as Margaret McMillan, are still familiar names today. Some less well-known figures who had an impact on developments in their day, such as Bertha Ronge and Katharine Bathurst, have been the subject of academic study. There are many who have not achieved even that modest fame. I believe that James Buchanan played a more important role in the development of the school at New Lanark, where he was the teacher, than his employer Robert Owen, who wrote the books and got the credit. I would have liked to say more than there was space for in a book of this size about the work of other people who are largely forgotten.

Conclusion

The first seven chapters of this book cover the history of early childhood services in more or less chronological order, but with an increasing amount of detail as we approach the present day. The last two main chapters invite you to reflect on that story and especially on the developments that took place during the period 1997–2010 when the Labour Party was in power and brought about significant changes in early years policy.

I appreciate that many readers will have only a limited idea of what happened in history over the last five hundred years and I have written this account of early childhood services with that in mind. In the first few chapters, which deal with the more remote past, I have included information on some of the general political and social background in boxes inserted in the text. I have also added a timeline at the end of the book that I hope will make the sequence of events clearer. There are suggestions for further reading at the end of most chapters for those who want to go into the history in more detail. The first seven chapters also end with exercises that invite you to consider one or more of the issues that have been raised.

There is more that could be usefully written about the ways in which early childhood services have developed, how these help explain the present and what they suggest might be possible in the future. In the meanwhile I hope this book will help you to grasp the overall story and appreciate its interest.

1 The birth of early childhood services (1500–1870)

The idea that the state should accept greater responsibility for children was hard at first for people to accept. Much was left to charitable effort. In the nineteenth century the most salient issue was the question of whether education should be provided for poorer children. Although there were initiatives of other kinds, it is with schools for infants that the history of early childhood services begins in earnest.

This chapter describes:

- the ways in which views on childhood and on the state's responsibilities for children's welfare began to change from the sixteenth to the nineteenth century;
- how urbanization and industrialization in the first 70 years of the nineteenth century led to initiatives by individuals and voluntary organizations with some support by government;
- influences on the education of young children in that period.

Developments in the sixteenth and seventeenth centuries

In the Middle Ages the Church was the principal body that assumed responsibility for children that their families could not meet. The Reformation and the religious disputes that followed disrupted, without closing down entirely, the social role of the established Church. As a result, secular authorities began, quite slowly, to assume the task. For example, it was in 1536 that the law on vagrancy first took into account the need to provide services for children without parents or whose parents were incapable of supporting them. Towards the end of the next century the Justices in Middlesex took the novel step of establishing an orphanage for their county (L'Estrange, 1686).

HISTORY IN A NUTSHELL

The Reformation

In the late Middle Ages the Papacy dominated religious institutions, but its considerable power was often criticized and led to clashes with rulers. There were also protests against the local clergy in many countries, including England, where the movement known as the 'Lollards' survived persecution and still operated in an underground manner in the early sixteenth century. In Germany, Martin Luther wanted to reform the Church by reducing the powers of the clergy rather than initiate a secular society (hence the term 'Reformation'). In England, the breach with the Papacy started, not with specifically religious notions, but with the political difficulties caused by Henry VIII's failure to produce a legitimate male heir – something that threatened the country with a return to the civil wars of the fifteenth century. The king rejected the right of the Pope to prevent the divorce and remarriage he hoped would solve his problem. The Tudor monarchs were, however, fairly conservative in matters of religion. Under Queen Mary there was even a return to Catholicism. Elizabeth managed a compromise on religious issues between Catholicism and the extreme forms of Protestantism. This left the Church with a major say in schooling for some time to come.

In sixteenth- and seventeenth-century England, a basic education was offered in 'petty schools' under the direction of local clergymen. These schools took younger children, sometimes children surprisingly young. Among those who were later to become famous and who started full-time education well before the age of 5 were Thomas Hobbes in 1592 and John Evelyn in 1624. Mulcaster, a leading sixteenth-century teacher and educational theorist, believed that no standard age should be set for children starting school. Their parents knew their abilities, personalities and stamina better than anyone else and for that reason should make the decision, although they should also seek advice before doing so (Mulcaster, 1581). For a long time there was little intervention by the state in education at the national level in England. There were, however, philanthropic initiatives on a local level. The first charity school in England opened as early as 1678.

Mulcaster's contribution to the debate as to when schooling should start was just one of many. It was recognized across Europe that the seventh birthday marked (approximately) a significant turning point in the life of a child – a view that still prevails in much of Europe. There was less agreement on the practical implications. Catholic countries tended to allow the Church at least as much responsibility as the parents for the moral and intellectual upbringing of the child. Protestants usually believed that children should be kept at home until 7 and expected parents to assume full responsibility for their care and education. The most influential statement of this point of view was that of the Czech theologian and educationist Comenius, who in 1633 defined four stages of education, the first of which he called 'the school of the mother' (Comenius, 1956).

Developments in the eighteenth century

In England the disruption of the Church's role in social affairs by the Civil War (1642–46) and its aftermath inhibited the creation of a system of basic schooling, such as Scotland enjoyed from the late seventeenth century onwards. Schooling was usually regarded as the privilege of a minority. More children attended school in the sixteenth century than did so two centuries later. When action was taken to increase the availability of schools towards the end of the eighteenth century, fears were expressed that this would spread unreasonable aspirations among the poor and encourage rebellion (Lawson and Silver, 1973: 234–5).

The ability of mothers to follow the advice of Comenius and other Protestant thinkers on their role in the early education of their children depended on their husbands having sufficient income for them to dispense with the need to earn money themselves. The effort that some mothers invested in the task of child-rearing became apparent in 1986 when scholars discovered a vast collection of books, toys and other items produced for her children by an early eighteenth-century vicar's wife in Lincolnshire (Brice Heath, 1997; Watson, 1997). As the eighteenth century progressed, commercial enterprises produced increasing numbers of books and other items for mothers in the wealthier sections of society to assist them in the task of educating their young.

In spite of this, there was still little appreciation of the learning potential of the youngest children or of their need for more than physical care. The first commercially produced toys alleged to have an educational purpose were designed for older children. The best-selling manual for household servants published by Hannah Woolley in 1670, and going through several editions clear into the eighteenth century, assumed that nothing much in the way of skills and only assiduous attention to duty were required of the maid who cared for very young children in a wealthy family.

Had Britain made industrial and economic progress more slowly than it did, the development of ideas about the care and education of young children might have continued at a steady rate. The beginnings of mass urbanization changed the picture.

Children and care outside the family home in the newly urbanized society of nineteenth-century England

Families in pre-industrial society often worked as units of production, although not with husbands and wives as equal partners. Childcare was fitted into that pattern. Well into the twentieth century it was still known in rural areas for women and older children to help out at key times, such as harvest, while the youngest children played near their mothers, penned in safely with the kind of portable fencing also used to keep farm animals secure (Abbott, 2003: 131). As urbanization progressed, the idea of the husband dealing with the wider world while his wife managed the household spread from the more affluent to the new working class. In Mrs Gaskell's 1848 novel, *Mary Barton*, two working-class characters condemn the employment of women in Manchester's factories. Young girls will spend their wages on frivolities and be led into sexual misdemeanours. Married women will have to neglect their husbands who will, as a result, be driven to the public house and alcoholism. It is interesting that the impact on children – the subject that was to seem most crucial to later generations – goes without mention. Mrs Gaskell was sufficiently well informed to know that it was a small minority of mothers of young children (as opposed to women in general) who sought employment outside the home.

Even so, there were few working-class families living in conditions that allowed them to follow the model of the home as a refuge from the grim world of paid employment. All children, including those who had loving parents, were likely to spend a lot of time outside the cramped room or cellar where they lived. Many lacked such care. In his novel *Sybil* (published in 1845, but set a few years earlier), Disraeli describes the childhood of Devilsdust, an otherwise nameless boy, abandoned by his mother and foster carer, growing up and surviving on his own. Such children represented an extreme, but many more probably spent a lot of time caring for themselves, learning only street wisdom and posing a potential nuisance to the adult world.

Some children spent a little time in what were commonly called dame schools (or later minding schools). These had started in the eighteenth century when the Church neglected the provision of basic education. In the early nineteenth century they became essentially a form of day care, although the women who ran them usually taught something in the way of literacy or sewing. Those who wanted a better 'system' of early education had little time for dame schools. A report by the Manchester Statistical Society published in 1834 was highly critical of them. On the other hand, a report by a similar body in Birmingham in 1838 speaks of the dame schools there as being 'much more satisfactory than could have been anticipated' (Thompson, 1988: 142–3).

A VOICE FROM THE TIME

The Manchester Statistical Society's opinion of dame schools

The greater part of them are kept by females, but some by older men whose only qualification for this kind of employment seems to be their unfitness for every other . . . the children go to be taken care of and to be kept out of the way at home. The dame schools are generally found in close, damp cellars or old dilapidated garrets . . . Occasionally, in some of the more respectable districts there are still to be found one or two of the old primitive dame schools, kept by a tidy elderly female, whose school has an appearance of neatness and order.

It is difficult to know whether Manchester and Birmingham were really different or whether the two societies were judging by different standards. Charles Dickens, who was always quick to denounce what he saw as abuses of children, paints a fairly positive picture of a minding school in his 1865 novel *Our Mutual Friend*. Betty Higden, who runs it, restricts herself to minding a handful of children so as to be able to conduct her laundry service safely at the same time. She is fond of the children and encourages her assistant to make them toys. No doubt she would be rated 'unsatisfactory' by a twenty-first-century childcare inspector, but by the standards of her own time she is doing an honest job. It is at least possible that her minding school was more typical than those denounced by the authors of the Manchester report.

It might be noted that while wealthier people commented on the irresponsibility of mothers who left their children with neighbours in order to work in the factories, they also relied on others for childcare. The period saw the rise of the nanny, a servant looking after children who was mid-way in status between the governess and the low-paid maid. By the 1860s even the wives of 'genteel tradesmen' expected to have the support of nannies (Perkin, 1993: 16). By the early twentieth century journalists were talking of the 'Kensington cripples', children from affluent families so used to the attentions of servants that they could not cope with simple tasks.

Early day care ventures

Some commentators were sympathetic to mothers who felt obliged to seek work and distanced themselves from the majority perspective, which was hostile. There is some evidence that factory owners regarded women with children as more highly motivated and, therefore, more reliable than younger women and encouraged them to return to work soon after childbirth (Perkin, 1993: 191). As early as 1835 the Fox Brothers opened a nursery in their factory in Somerset. Thirty years later they replaced the building they had first used with one that was purpose-built (Briggs, 1978: 11–12). There was a flurry of such activity in 1850. In March of that year a group of ladies, inspired by reports of provision in Paris, opened a nursery in Marylebone in London. Others followed. By the end of the nineteenth century day care was usually seen as a way of meeting the needs of less able mothers. The mid-century day nurseries, on the other hand, only accepted those they considered to be responsible parents and required from applicants for places recommendations from clergymen or other gentlemen and proof that their children were healthy. The idea of day care spread from the capital. Towards the end of 1850 Mrs Clements, the wife of a local vicar, opened a day nursery in Halstead, a manufacturing town in Essex. The area where the greatest number of initiatives was taken was Lancashire. The first of these was in the working-class neighbourhood of Ancoats in Manchester. The attendance of the Bishop and the Lord Mayor at the ceremony to open the nursery there demonstrated the approval of the most important figures in the city.

All these early ventures came up against the problem that their promoters expected them to be financially self-sufficient. This just did not happen. The fees were too high for most families. Mrs Clements closed her nursery three years after it opened. The one in Ancoats closed shortly afterwards.

Interest in the education of the urban poor

The idea of day care met with less success than the idea of infant education. Several politicians believed that the proper response to the problems of the expanding cities might entail more than deploying troops to put down disorder. They were aware of experiments that had taken place in various European countries under the patronage of Oberlin, Fellenberg and others. The end of the wars with Napoleon's France in 1815 made it easier for the wealthy and the curious to visit some of these experiments.

HISTORY IN A NUTSHELL

The wars with France

In 1789 a revolution began in France. At first, many of the upper classes in England were sympathetic, seeing what was happening there as the rejection of an autocratic, Catholic monarchy. They believed it was essentially similar to the 'Glorious Revolution' in England in 1688 that had led to the deposition of James II. Later, and especially after the execution of the French king, most of them opposed what was happening. Fears that the new French government would prove to be as dangerous an enemy as French kings had often been led England into war with France, which continued (with one brief interval) after the republic was replaced by Napoleon Bonaparte's 'Empire'. The wars ended with Napoleon's final defeat at Waterloo in 1815. The end of the war brought economic difficulties that particularly affected the urban poor as demand for military equipment fell drastically.

Inspired by foreign examples, a movement began for the greater provision of schools for young children. Joseph Lancaster, who had opened a school for poor children in 1798, became famous for devising a form of industrial production in schooling. In 1804 he started a school in Southwark with eight hundred pupils (soon rising to a thousand) where older pupils acted as 'monitors' to their younger peers (an early form of cascade training). He travelled around England to spread this idea and secured royal patronage. In 1816 he made the mistake of becoming entangled in a rancorous disagreement with other leading figures in the society he had founded to promote his ideas and walked out on it. This was the first of many ugly squabbles between advocates of early education that soured things in England over the next hundred years or more. His influence declined after that.

The career of Samuel Wilderspin

Following the split in what had been the Royal Lancasterian Society, Lord Brougham and some of his friends made a fresh attempt to launch non-denominational schools for young children. The first was an infant school in Brewer's Green in London. A second was opened in Quaker Street in Spitalfields with Samuel Wilderspin, a former Sunday School teacher, at its head. These infant schools were intended for children from as young as 18 months, which is why the infant school movement must be seen as a significant part of the history of early childhood services. Wilderspin's approach to education did not go down well with many of the working-class parents who sent their children to him. They complained that he was not teaching them to read and write as quickly as they wished. Children were withdrawn, but numbers picked up after a while as it became apparent that his approach really did help children to learn. This did not assuage all his critics. As his career progressed, Wilderspin was often accused by Evangelical Christians of allowing too much room for 'amusement' in the infant schools he created. They found more to admire in the approach to 'nursery discipline' outlined by Louisa Howe in a book first published in 1814 that proved so popular it went into many editions and was still selling well in the 1840s.

Wilderspin is a controversial figure. Like Lancaster, he thought well of himself and claimed to have invented a whole system of infant education that fitted the needs of his age. It is not easy to assess how original a thinker he was. Certainly the book that he regarded as his most important publication *A System for the Education of the Young* (1840) asks a lot of the reader. It is a confusing mix of observations on school management, accounts of his own travels to promote infant education and a large number of what are, in effect, lesson plans that seem to lend themselves too easily to the worst kind of what he himself called 'parrot work'.

He has been condemned in recent years on two counts: corporal punishment and hyper-discipline. In spite of the contrary views of his patrons, such as Brougham, he was prepared when he first started to resort to corporal punishment. He felt obliged to defend himself against the 'strictures' of the *Edinburgh Review* on this score in an appendix to the second edition of his book *The Importance of Educating the Infant Poor* (Wilderspin, 1824). He was particularly sensitive to the criticism that corporal punishment had not been found necessary in the school in Robert Owen's experimental community at New Lanark. He believed his critics failed to recognize the nature of what had happened there. New Lanark was a highly structured community where factory, homes and school were all provided under a single plan. In that context an invisible discipline was in place. He, on the other hand, had to keep control in a school situated in a highly disorganized neighbourhood and this excused resort to force. In all probability most of the parents who sent their children to his school would have found this understandable. Wilderspin abandoned the use of corporal punishment in time.

The other criticism is that his design of schools and the way that lessons were conducted were hyper-disciplined. Again, he saw this as essential if children were to benefit from periods in school that might prove very brief.

FIGURES OF THE TIME

Robert Owen, 1771–1858

Born in Wales, Owen became a successful industrialist. He was, however, concerned at the growing rift in society between businessmen and the urban poor. In 1799 he acquired property, including the cotton mill, at New Lanark that he turned into a model of the new industrial society he wanted to see, supplying the workers and their families with various services at his own expense. He became famous in 1813 when he wrote about his experience in his book *A New View of Society*. The infant school at New Lanark became an inspiring example. It is a matter of controversy how many of the ideas about the way the school should be run were Owen's own. He had at least the intelligence to articulate the approach adopted there (which included an absolute prohibition on corporal punishment). A hundred years later he was often described as one of the first socialists. He was more important as someone who popularized the concept of ideal, small-scale communities. He was a model for later industrialists who built small towns, such as Saltaire and Bourneville, to demonstrate what a harmonious industrial society might be like.

Henry Brougham, 1778–1868

Born and educated in Edinburgh, Brougham practised as a lawyer there and later in London. In 1810 he entered the House of Commons. He had a brief period in office from 1830 to 1834 (when he became Baron Brougham & Vaux), but was best known as an advocate of advanced opinions. He was, for example, a leading figure in the anti-slavery movement. He also had a long-standing interest in education and tried to secure legislation on the matter in 1837. However, he opposed any compulsory state system of schooling. He was an important patron of various attempts to establish infant schools, especially in London.

Several things can be said about Wilderspin. He recognized the importance of children learning from experience and from physical contact with things as well as verbal constructs. He saw the value of free play, especially outdoors. He recognized the importance of observing what children did, especially outside formal lessons, and, in doing so, anticipated ideas that were to be elaborated by others after him.

Wilderspin's appreciation of free play

The pupils being supplied with the necessary articles for amusement, the teacher must not fail to remember that the choice is always left to the children. If they play at what they choose, they are free beings and manifest their characters, but if they are forced to play at what they do not wish, they do not manifest their characters, but are cramped and are slaves and hence their faculties are not developed.

Source: (Wilderspin, 1824: xi)

Above all, the energy he put into starting new infant schools is more than impressive. He outdid Lancaster in his travels and propaganda. He visited most parts of England, much of Scotland and various parts of Wales and Ireland. He was open-minded in his efforts to establish working relationships with fiercely Evangelical Protestants in Scotland and Lancashire and (even less successfully) with Catholics in Ireland. By 1836 he calculated that 270 infant schools had been established mainly by his efforts. He was still at work in the 1840s when he set up a school in Barton-upon-Humber.

The greater readiness of government to intervene

Wilderspin and others had an enthusiastic following, but not universal approval. In Disraeli's *Sybil* (1845), Lady Marney takes a benevolent interest in early education for the poor, but her son Lord Marney expresses an 'imperious hope that no infant school would ever be found in his neighbourhood'. Both support and opposition were most often expressed at local level, but eventually the work of voluntary societies and charismatic individuals prompted action by central government.

As early as 1811 there had been a government inquiry into the 'Education of the Lower Orders' in London and a similar inquiry covering the rest of Britain followed in 1818. In 1833 the first government grants to schools were made (initially for buildings only, later for furniture and equipment). The Poor Law of 1834 made provision for schools in workhouses. The pace of change quickened when the Privy Council established a Committee on Education and appointed the first schools inspectors in 1839. Another significant step took place in 1846 when the government oversaw the replacement of Lancaster's monitorial system with one of pupil-teachers (older pupils undertaking a form of apprenticeship). Grants for schools were followed in 1854 by grants for courses of study for those who wanted to be infant school teachers. Three years later scholarships for pupil-teachers were established. In 1862 the government introduced a system of payment of grants to schools on the basis of results (an early version of target setting and league tables, but one that entailed even more pressure on teachers to groom pupils for inspection in order to secure their own continued employment).

These were all significant extensions of the power and responsibility of government. There were those who wanted to go further, but their ideas had little support at least in the political establishment. The Chartists, a radical political movement, produced proposals for state intervention in education (Lovett and Collins, 1841), but these faded from view with the collapse of that movement. A more modest, but more detailed, attempt to extend state involvement came in the 1850s when leaders of Lancashire's industrial and merchant class put forward a parliamentary bill. They proposed that the new municipal authorities in Manchester and Salford (created along with other new local authorities by the Municipal Corporations Act of 1835) should establish their own school system. Opposition killed the bill. One critic warned that, if successful, the proposed scheme would damage moves to set up infant schools on a voluntary organization basis, deprive parents of their rights, encourage a detached perspective on religion and facilitate moves to despotic government through the influence state employees would have on children (Giles, 1852). Similar arguments are, of course, made today by those who want to break up the system of local authority-controlled schools that was later established.

HISTORY IN A NUTSHELL

The Chartists

In 1832 an Act was passed making several reforms in the way the House of Commons was elected. A good deal of hope had been invested in this change and, as it became apparent that the reforms were modest and that the conditions of the urban poor were worsening, demands grew for further reform. In 1838 radical leaders composed a 'charter' outlining proposals for more radical changes in the parliamentary system. This was presented to Parliament and rejected in 1839. Two further presentations of the demands were also rejected in 1842 and 1848. In 1848 there were attempted revolutions in several parts of Europe and similar violence was anticipated in England, with the charter providing a rallying point. The revolution did not happen and Chartism as a movement was dead ten years later. When it died, it was growing prosperity rather than repression by the state that killed it.

Factors in thinking about education

By the late 1860s the majority of children in England aged 3 to 11 years received some form of schooling, although the quality and length of time at school varied considerably. The pedagogical theory that was available was relatively undeveloped. Lancaster's monitorial system was intended to make schools cheaper and entailed little consideration of the ways in which children learn. Wilderspin had some ideas of his own, but he was not very good at getting them down on paper.

The impact of phrenology

There were some influences on thinking about education that would be very unfamiliar now, including phrenology, an early attempt at scientific psychology (de Giustino, 1975). The claim made by phrenology's adherents was that individual personality traits and abilities revealed themselves in the precise shape of the skull. The expert phrenologist would feel the top of someone's head and pronounce on his character. The fact that this idea was taken seriously is usually shrugged off now as an oddity of former times. In fact, the phrenologists were onto something. It was just that, in the absence of the sort of brain-imaging techniques available today, they were looking in the wrong place for clues to the physical basis of personality, examining the surface of the head rather than its internal organization. The idea that the individual mind is not ready made, but is a combination of specific domains within the brain that come together in some way to generate the subjective experience of a single consciousness is now an important influence on thinking about early cognitive development (Karmilov-Smith, 1992). Phrenology was premature rather than bizarre. In the 1820s many of those involved in infant education were impressed by it. Wilderspin described himself as a 'semi-convert'. He saw that it might provide a scientific under-pinning for his own instinct that education should be based on a variety of forms of learning. When he used the phrase 'for all the faculties' in the title of his major work he was signalling clearly to his contemporaries that he believed in a form of education that took what today's neuro-psychologists call 'modularity' into account, but went beyond it.

The religious dimension of disputes about government's role in schools

Religion was an even more important factor. The main reason for the sustained opposition to state-sponsored schooling was that Anglicans and Protestants outside the Anglican Church (the 'dissenters' as they were usually known) were both afraid that they would lose influence if they did not have their own schools. Similar issues arose in Ireland and in parts of Scotland and Lancashire in relation to Roman Catholicism, but these difficulties did not have the same impact on the debate on schooling or the development of government policy. Throughout the nineteenth century the British and Foreign Schools Society (created by dissenters out of the ruins of the Royal Lancasterian Society) and the National Society for Promoting the Education of the Poor (which promoted schools loyal to the Church of England) wielded powerful influence over politicians. Both organizations secured concessions for themselves that limited the grip of the Privy Council's Committee on Education. They also opposed moves towards non-denominational schooling. The religious issue continued to dominate political discussion about schools well into the twentieth century. It had an impact difficult to appreciate today, inhibiting those at the forefront of educational reform. Kay-Shuttleworth, the central figure in the Committee on Education when it was first established, seems to have lived in constant fear of his political enemies being able to make something of the fact that many of his extended family were Unitarians, that is to say, people who denied the orthodox doctrine of the Trinity (Selleck, 1994: 151–2). His anxieties on that score undermined his willingness to press for non-denominational schooling.

In the context of rivalry between Anglicans and dissenters the push for more educational provision for children of the urban working class usually came from politicians with no strong commitment (in spite of their nominal membership) to the established Church. They were able to take a detached view because they were children of the Enlightenment, interested in religion mainly as a way of bolstering morality and the social order. A different contribution came from those who belonged to minority Churches – Swedenborgians, Quakers, Unitarians and Moravians. Of those groups the Swedenborgians (or the Church of the New Jerusalem, as they called themselves) were by far the most important in the spread of the infant school movement. James Buchanan (the teacher at New Lanark), Samuel Wilderspin and other significant figures, such as David Goyder, were all converts to Swedenborgianism. Their minority faith placed them to one side of the conflicts between the major denominations and able to focus on a non-sectarian view of what a school system should entail. It also opened up a more optimistic view of childhood than was found in orthodox theology. Swedenborg's belief that each child had inherited dispositions to evil, but was nevertheless able to respond to the good, made respect for the child's own attempts at understanding possible. This perspective on early childhood was one of the themes in the influential summary of Swedenborg's ideas published by the Rev. Joseph Proud (1810). It encouraged ideas about supporting children's own learning rather than just teaching them.

Today the religious dimension of the mindset of many of the pioneers of early childhood education is easily overlooked. Faith is often seen as an obstacle to progress or, at best, as providing the motivation of some individuals, but having little other interest. This makes it all too easy to misunderstand the process of change itself. Moreover, ideas like those of Swedenborg continued to have influence well into the twentieth century. *New Era*, the journal of the Theosophical Society, carried numerous articles about progressive ideas in education in the 1920s. Piaget, whose ideas were highly influential on education in the latter part of the twentieth century, had been a leading figure in the liberal Protestant movement in his native Switzerland while he was still a student. His first publications were theological rather than scientific and the ideas in those essays strongly influenced his early book *The Moral Judgement of the Child* (Vidal, 1987). It is easy to see a parallel between Piaget's view of the relationship between teacher and child and the Protestant rejection of priesthood in favour of a more limited, though still significant, role for ministers of religion.

Concepts of education

This brief overview of the influence of both phrenology and minority religious faiths is enough to demonstrate that the movement for early childhood education in the first half of the nineteenth century was influenced by specific ideas. It would be wrong to suggest that the focus was entirely on getting as much teaching done as possible without considering how children's learning could best be supported. However, it was in other parts of Europe that ideas on the nature of early education really had their origin. Maria Edgeworth, daughter of a leading Irish writer on education, wrote a novel that was a thinly disguised account of the work Mme. de Pastoret carried out at infant schools in Paris. The French educationist reciprocated by taking up some of Wilderspin's ideas and becoming one of the first to spread his fame in Europe. The work of Pestalozzi was also influential thanks mainly to a translation by J.P. Greaves of letters on early education that Pestalozzi had written to him. The British and Foreign Schools Society adopted many of Pestalozzi's ideas on the teaching of numeracy (a subject that was comfortably neutral from a theological perspective). Several schools claimed to be 'Pestalozzian' and Greaves collaborated with Wilderspin in the writing of one of his books (McCann and Young, 1982: 64–5). However, it is arguable that the school opened by Synge in County Wicklow in Ireland early in the nineteenth century was the only one in the United Kingdom to be established on lines that Pestalozzi himself would have approved.

The influence of Froebel in England

The decisive influence from abroad came in the second half of the nineteenth century – that of the followers of Froebel. One reason for this was that several of Froebel's followers had to seek asylum in England from repressive regimes in Germany after the failed revolutions of 1848. Since there is nothing in Froebel's thought that clearly aligns him with the political left, some have been puzzled by the hostility shown towards him by the authorities in Germany. His school ventures were subject to a number of investigations by state officials. The inspectors were often positively impressed by what they saw. In spite of this, the Prussian government banned the kindergarten system in 1851. This was not mere obscurantism. They had some reason to see what was happening as a threat to the established order. In particular, they were worried by the Women's College that Froebel's nephew helped to set up in Berlin in 1849 and by the enthusiasm that followers of Froebel, such as Baroness von Marenholtz-Bülow, showed for 'woman's educational mission' (von Marenholtz-Bülow, 1855). The Prussian authorities considered the possibility of middle-class ladies entering paid professions, such as teaching, to be as much a threat to the values of the regime as university students hurling cobblestones at policemen in the street.

When several of Froebel's female disciples came to England they joined the middle-class German communities that were already well established in London and Manchester. The spread of the kindergarten movement took place initially within those communities. It is interesting that, while the term 'kindergarten' has been translated into the local language in France, Spain and other European countries, it has retained its German form in Britain. In 1851 Mr and Mrs Ronge opened a kindergarten in Hampstead, a middle-class neighbourhood in London. At first the setting took only the children of German immigrants. It soon received its first English pupils, the sons of Frederic Hill who had argued in 1836 that the children of middle-class families were as much in need of early education as the children of the poor. In 1854 one of the official school inspectors wrote enthusiastically about the kindergarten he had visited, which 'treats the child as a child, encourages it to think for itself' (Wood, 1934: 12). In 1855 Bertha Ronge published a book in English explaining Froebel's ideas and another author translated a similar book by Baroness von Marenholtz-Bülow. Wider publicity followed when Charles Dickens published articles praising this approach in two of the country's leading magazines.

In 1857 a Miss Barton opened the first kindergarten in Manchester and a committee was set up in the city to promote the kindergarten concept. Others settings were established between 1860 and 1862 (Wood, 1934: 19). However, in an unpleasant repeat of what had happened to Joseph Lancaster earlier in the century, several local supporters of the kindergarten movement began a whisper against Bertha Ronge, claiming that she was an advocate of 'free thinking'. She left Manchester for Europe the following year. The dispute was damaging, but the movement itself expanded even further in the following decades and become a major source of new ideas on what could be achieved in the field of early education.

Conclusion

The first seventy years of the nineteenth century saw the exponential spread of a movement to provide schooling for young children – one in which a focus on quantity had gradually been modified by ideas about the ways in which early education could best be conducted. The basis had also been laid for the development of a system of state education of a kind that had not been envisaged at the beginning of the century.

Exercise

Ask your local Development Education Centre for any material they have or can recommend on children in the new slums of major cities in Latin America, Africa or Asia. What does this suggest to you about the situation of the mass of young children in the expanding cities of this country at the start of the nineteenth century?

Further reading

The biography of Samuel Wilderspin by McCann and Young (1982) deals intelligently and comprehensively with one of the leading figures of the period.

Brehony's chapter in *Kindergartens and Cultures: The Global Diffusion of an Idea* (ed. R. Wollans, 2000) is an excellent account of the influence of Froebel in this country for the period covered by this chapter and the next.

The reader with a limited knowledge of history will find Black's *The Making of Modern Britain* (2001) a useful introduction.

2 The state's assumption of responsibility for early childhood services (1870–1945)

In the eighteenth century the responsibilities of government were not envisaged as stretching much beyond the protection of property from the threats posed by trading rivals and foreign monarchs abroad or the disaffected poor at home. The opportunities and difficulties created by industrialization and urbanization began to modify the picture in relation to basic education and other issues, such as public health, during the first seventy years or so of the nineteenth century. The period from 1870 to 1945 saw the consolidation of a new conception of the state and its responsibilities.

This chapter describes:

- some of the ways in which 1870 marked a significant turning point;
- the changing situation of women and children;
- the development of early education, nursery care, childminding, playwork and parent support in the period up until the Second World War;
- the impact of that war on family life and the provision of early childhood services.

The start of a new era

There was a significant shift in the development of the United Kingdom round about the year 1870. All attempts to define historical periods come up against the refusal of reality to fit neatly into chronological boxes. However, it is reasonable to see the years between 1870 and 1945 as constituting a single historical period.

HISTORY IN A NUTSHELL

Why the period around 1870 marked a crucial turning point in British history

A war between France and the German states in 1870 severely disrupted the French financial system. This led to the London stock exchange achieving greater international prominence.

This, in turn, gave London renewed vigour as the economic centre of the UK. The stock exchanges in the major industrial cities rapidly declined.

This reversed the situation earlier in the century when the emerging industrial cities established themselves as rival centres of political, economic and cultural power.

The new importance of the London stock exchange, together with the advantages of empire, helped to mask a slow decline in the relative importance of British large-scale industry as more nations caught up with and then overtook the UK in manufacturing capacity. Where there was innovation in industry, it was in specialized small-scale manufacturing, often outside the major northern cities in parts of the South of England.

The continuing improvements in agricultural techniques in the UK and elsewhere meant that reasonable quality food became more readily available. In real terms the price of food fell in the last decades of the nineteenth century.

This improved the standard of living of the majority of people. It initiated the situation we still have today where the larger part of the working population enjoys a degree of comfort (though one always threatened by recession), while a substantial minority of people live in a situation of permanent disadvantage, but are not driven to mass action by hunger.

Reform of the parliamentary system in 1867, 1884 and 1885 gave a more decisive voice in politics to the majority of the male population. (Women had to wait for the vote until after the First World War.)

These reforms encouraged the development of more highly organized political parties and led to the situation now considered normal whereby any party that comes to power after an election does so with a political and legislative programme in mind.

There were also significant improvements in the system of local government and local authorities began to take over crucial services.

The social, economic and political changes that happened around the year 1870 affected services for young children. In the seventy years or so that followed, the foundations were laid for government to take the lead role in education, including early education, and for the provision of new services in day care, child protection, playwork and support to mothers.

Much of this was positive. However, the development of specific services also led to what was later denounced as 'fragmentation'. In the earlier part of the nineteenth century those who wanted better for young children were concerned almost exclusively with schooling. After 1870 other agencies and professions began to emerge as different issues were identified. The creation of new structures in both central and local government helped to turn differences of focus into differences of institutional function. By the 1990s many saw the fragmentation of early childhood services as their crucial defect. In that context it was often forgotten that the creation of different areas of professional practice had been central to the development of provision in the period 1870–1945.

Before going on to discuss in detail developments in early education, day care, maternity and child welfare services and play, it is important to spell out some of the social and intellectual background – the changing situation of women and new ideas about children's cognitive and emotional development.

The changing situation of women

Industrialization had an important impact on women. Their status had long been one of subordination to men. In the nineteenth century that subordination was complicated and may have been worsened by the increasing separation of home and work. Expectations of the ideal wife and mother were created that many working-class families could not afford. The employment of women in manufacturing varied from place to place, depending on the type of industry, but was still significant. Some found ways of gaining income while staying at home. Mothers who did not go out to work might undertake needlework, laundry services, running a small shop from the front room, providing childcare for neighbours. For a large number of working-class women the question just did not arise, as they worked in domestic service where conditions of service precluded normal family life.

Husbands from the middle and upper classes could afford to keep their wives and daughters out of paid employment, but towards the end of the nineteenth century there were challenges to this practice. Bella in *Our Mutual Friend* declared her intention to be 'something so much worthier than the doll in the doll's house' (Dickens, 1865). In the years that followed, her cry was taken up by increasing numbers of people more in sympathy with it than Dickens himself. The Society for Promoting the Employment of Women had already been launched in 1859. Like many of the organizations interested in 'the woman question' (Stanton, 1884), its main concern was with women from the wealthier and better educated parts of society. That included some 75,000 'ladies of rank and property' in the early 1870s who had no paid occupation but were single and likely to remain so (Hobsbawm, 1969: 119). Single status, whether freely chosen or imposed by circumstance, in combination with adequate income, freed women to play a part in public life. If a woman married, she subordinated herself to her husband and was likely to spend much of her married life giving birth to and caring for children. If she looked for sexual relationships outside marriage, she risked the respectable status on which her public activity depended. It was only close to the start of the twentieth century that some women (such as Beatrice Webb, Emily Ward and Katherine Bruce Glasier) found husbands happy to support their public activity. Mrs Pankhurst's campaign for votes for women did not begin until after her husband had died.

Because the idea of women entering paid employment challenged conventional opinion, they often sought work in areas that reflected their traditional role as carers, such as nursing or the teaching of young children. In the twentieth century whole areas of paid employment came to be seen as 'women's work', sometimes in ways that had not been anticipated. Sales assistants in the larger retail outlets and secretarial and other clerical staff had been almost exclusively men at the start of the twentieth century, but were normally women by the 1950s. Entirely new occupations were captured by women. Telephone operators (in the days before automated exchanges) were all women from the start. The compromise that allowed women into the male world of work at the price of carving out a limited number of jobs as somehow especially theirs (and often poorly paid) was successful, but it reinforced as much as it undermined the earlier model of woman's role in society.

A parallel development occurred in working-class politics. Gallagher (1977) describes the way in which activism among working-class women in the 1970s was often not the result of a feminist rejection of their domestic role, but of anger at the obstacles that hindered them in undertaking it. This had been true for a long time. In the 1790s women had rioted in protest against government failure to provide the bread they needed for their children. The Tenants Defence Leagues of the English Midlands in the 1880s, the 1915 Rent Strike in Glasgow and the widespread rent strikes on English council estates in the 1960s were all instances of social movements concerned with preserving the family home in which women played the leading role, sometimes in the teeth of fierce resentment from men.

The ambiguities in the struggle of women to gain new footholds in the sphere of paid employment also affected some of the moves to create new services for young children. Those who demanded such reforms often did so in the name of their duty as women. 'Social maternalism' was a significant element in the developing teaching profession (Lewis, 1984: 92–7; Brehony, 1999). This helps to explain political alliances that might otherwise seem surprising, such as that between Margaret McMillan, a member of the Independent Labour Party, and Lady Astor, the leading Conservative, in the demand for more nursery schools in the 1920s. It is also reflected in some more recent developments, such as the joint management of a childcare project in Bristol by the Women's Royal Voluntary Service, that pillar of the establishment, and Gingerbread, the militant campaigning organization for single parents.

Changing attitudes to childhood

The twin processes of urbanization and industrialization, which altered the situation of women, had a related impact on children. The reason was essentially the same – that children were removed to a large extent from material production. Childhood became simultaneously a comfortable place protected from the wider world and a time of preparation for that world.

The previous chapter spoke of the beginnings of literature specifically aimed at children in the eighteenth century. This development continued and the half-century before the First World War is often spoken of as the 'Golden Age' of children's literature. This was part of a wider alteration in the way that childhood was perceived. Zeliger (1985) claims there was a profound transformation in the value people in Europe and America placed, not just on their own children, but on children in general. The previous three hundred years or so had seen a grudging willingness on the part of the state to assume some responsibility for children whose parents were absent or were unable to provide their care. A wider responsibility for children now became politically acceptable.

Earlier in the nineteenth century the principal reason for the interest some took in the children of the working class was the desire to steer them away from crime and revolution. A few individuals also recognized that the emerging industrial society required a greater proportion of the population to be responsible citizens who were literate and numerate and, perhaps, had undertaken formal occupational training (although Britain was never as clear about the importance of vocational education as some other European countries, with consequences with which we are still living). Both these considerations lay behind the infant school movement. A concentration on education characterized concern for the nation's children. In the last part of the nineteenth century and well into the twentieth century new problems were taken into account. Greater understanding of infection forced politicians to appreciate that the insanitary conditions of the poor threatened the health of their betters. Attachment to empire and fear of the rising power of newly united Germany created pressure to ensure that the country had enough fit young men to defend it. Health came to dominate concerns about children. In 1800 no one would have suggested that doctors had any special expertise to bring to bear on the subject of child-rearing. By 1900 that proposition was universally accepted.

The involvement of doctors was associated with a turn from theology and towards science in the conception of childhood. The approaches to education developed by the pioneers had been based to a significant extent on religious values, instinct and practical experience. Demand grew for a more rigorous approach. One of the leading theorists of education in the period after the First World War accepted that nineteenth-century ideas on education had much to recommend them, but criticized them for not being 'based on facts of child life ascertained by direct observation and experiment' (Fynne, 1924: 6). This was a new perspective.

The idea that direct observation and experiment were essential to understanding young children came from what might seem at first a surprising source – concern for children with disabilities. To an extent that is often unrecognized, modern pedagogical theory was built on work with children with special educational needs. Many leading figures, such as Montessori and Vygotsky, developed their views on education while working with children with learning difficulties. It was the challenge that such children posed that led them to rethink standard approaches.

This started even earlier. In the late eighteenth century, Pereira, a Spaniard living in France, devoted his life to the education of deaf mutes. He was possibly the first person in the world to do so. He developed a teaching system based on close observation of individual children and the use of touch to help them understand their own vocal cords and thus develop some form of speech. His work impressed Séguin, a later specialist in the field of disability, who published an appreciation of him in 1847. Séguin also came to the radical conclusion that it was possible to teach children with serious learning difficulties as well as those with physical disabilities (Séguin, 1846). He believed this could be done if traditional teaching methods based exclusively on language were modified and practitioners learned through observation how children managed to develop their own understanding of the world through what Bruner (1966) would later describe as 'enactive representation'. He went further and claimed that pedagogy that worked with 'idiots' (the technical term at the time for people with learning difficulties) would also work well with other children. His most important book, which he published in English after moving to the United States, further underlined this assertion and challenged conventional notions of teaching by describing passive deference to the authority of the teacher as a mistake (Séguin, 1866).

In the twentieth century Séguin's ideas were taken up by Margaret McMillan and Maria Montessori. Those two were also influenced by the German author Preyer, whose book *Die Seele des Kindes* (1882) was one of the first systematic studies of children's cognitive development and remained an influential text for several decades. He helped dismantle the eighteenth-century notion that a child's mind was a blank page on which the adult had to write the information the child needed to understand the world. Long before the modern science of genetics was established (although the idea was in the air) Preyer argued that children were born with different abilities and that observation and experiment might show how these were developing and guide parental or pedagogical support.

Thus the scientific study of children with disabilities began to lead into research on cognitive development some thirty years before Piaget's innovative studies. James Sully's influential *Studies of Childhood* (1895) took the study of child development in this country even further forward. With the impact of psychoanalysis in the 1920s and 1930s attention turned to the emotional development of the child in the work of Melanie Klein and others (Riley, 1983: 62–84). The fact that she ran a school for a while and later wrote a regular advice column for *Nursery* World made the child psychologist Susan Isaacs a particularly important figure for those involved in early childhood services (Willan, 2009).

The periods before and after the First World War were, therefore, when ideas on child development and the application of these to education, were coming to the fore. After that war there were frequent disputes between those who supported new ideas in schools and those, like the politician Lord Eustace Percy, who dismissed them as 'romantic' (Whitbread, 1972: 94–5). This division of opinion is, of course, still with us. In 1925 Jessie Mackinder made the case for young children to be allowed to work in small groups within the larger classroom with the teacher available to help. Her book had the potential to kill off finally Lancaster's mass production approach. Instead it was nearly half a century before practice of the sort she described became commonplace and even then it had many people worried that this was not 'proper' teaching. Since early childhood provides the period in which cognitive and physical development are in many ways most obvious, and reliance on words as a means of teaching most clearly problematic, experiments in early education hastened the spread of innovative ideas about teaching. Jones (1924) was just one of several authors who drew attention to this connection. This was a consideration that led politicians and officials to have reservations about the enthusiasts for pre-school education.

A VOICE FROM THE TIME

The implications for education of the new appreciation of child development

Premature achievement does not make for sound growth nor for permanent gain. It often produces an outward appearance of growth without the reality – like flowers stuck in the sand that make a brave show

> momentarily and then wither and die. Failure to give the right opportunity for the full use of powers is equally wasteful and may cause an arrest in the growth of those powers.
>
> *Source*: (de Lissa, 1939: 4)

The elementary school

From 1815 to 1870 a large number of fee-paying schools, catering for children aged up to 7 were established by voluntary effort with some support from the state. They were supplemented by the 'ragged schools' provided free for the children of the very poor, the Sunday School movement and the small number of kindergartens in London, Manchester, Edinburgh and other cities.

An Education Act was passed in 1870, creating a system of local elementary schools throughout England and Wales. Legislation establishing a similar system in Scotland was passed in 1872. Later measures followed:

1871: a new Code for Schools separated out the teaching requirements for children aged 5–7 from those of older children, although it failed to take into account the fact that many schools had children aged under 5.

1876: attendance at school (or education at home) by children under 10 was made universally compulsory.

1881: the system of payment by results was finally dropped.

1891: school fees were abolished.

1895: the system of annual exams was replaced by a new schools inspection system.

1902: the local boards of education that had been established under the 1870 Act were abolished and their functions taken over by local authorities.

The abolition of school fees was especially indicative of changing attitudes. It made it easier for poor parents to comply with the requirement that their children attend school. It also entailed acceptance of the idea that the community as a whole had a responsibility for the education of children and could exercise it without undermining the role of parents.

The crucial decision made in 1870

In some respects the most important decision that was made was that compulsory education should begin at the age of 5 – something still in force today. The standard view across Europe was formal education should begin around the time of the seventh birthday. This remained true in Britain for a long time for those who could afford private education. 'Preparatory' schools usually took children at 7. Even in the 1930s it was still assumed by many middle-class people that formal education would not begin before the seventh birthday (Wynne, 1936). The decision to make the fifth rather than the seventh birthday the boundary point was not taken on grounds related to any theory of education. It seems to have been based on the view that the sooner the children of the working class had concluded elementary education and were ready for employment the better (Blackstone, 1971: 23). This view remains influential. We now assume that young people will stay in full-time education much later than was envisaged for the majority in 1870, but many politicians and parents (though not many people professionally engaged in early childhood education) still firmly believe that an early start is best.

Under-5s in the elementary schools and the concept of the nursery school

Apart from the failure to address pedagogical concerns when the decision was made, there was also a failure to consider what was already happening to children aged under 5. Large numbers of them were at school. Rules on compulsory attendance at school became increasingly strict over time and the abolition of school fees encouraged more parents to send their children aged 5 or over to school. The increase in the number of over-4s created considerable pressure to keep younger children out. There was just not enough room in the school buildings. Nevertheless, the elementary schools were widely used by parents of children under 5 who wanted to send them either because they agreed with the idea of starting formal education early or because they needed childcare or because they saw schools as healthier places for their children than the houses in which they lived.

The problem of accommodating the under-5s in the new elementary schools became critical. There was often too little space and too little understanding of child development for this to be done effectively. Briggs (1978: 25–7) describes the difficulties at the school of an impoverished mining village in Derbyshire in the 1860s. It had just one room for all children from babies to those at the end of elementary education. As well as finding it difficult to deal with the cramped conditions, teachers were clearly confused by the response of the youngest children and believed that, if they attended school, they should be able to cope with normal lessons. Briggs writes about a situation that existed just before the 1870 Act rather than after it, but the attitudes of which she speaks would have taken time to change.

Demands from parents that their under-5s should have places in the elementary schools continued. This was a problem for government right up until the 1930s, although the Cross Commission on Elementary Education had recognized the difficulty as early as 1886. It was sometimes argued that it was essential to provide space for the under-5s at school because otherwise their older sisters would be kept off school to look after them. Civil servants appreciated the dilemma but questioned whether the country could afford to accommodate large numbers of under-5s in school (Gordon et al., 1991: 158). In spite of the concerns, it would seem that some two-fifths of children aged 3 to 5 were attending school regularly at the start of the twentieth century.

In 1904 anxiety about the poor health of many prospective recruits to the army for a war in South Africa led to an Inter-Departmental Committee Report. Among other things this put the case for separate settings for under-5s. The following year a report by women inspectors at the Board of Education also suggested the need for such settings. Even before the official report was published one of the inspectors, Katharine Bathurst, had submitted a report of her own that was severely critical of existing provision and argued for kindergartens or at least for wholesale adoption of Froebelian principles wherever under-5s were accepted in elementary schools. She was forced to resign. The more moderate proposals of the official report were also rejected. Instead the Board of Education authorized local authorities to refuse admission of under-5s to elementary schools. By 1908 more than half of them had taken advantage of this.

The idea of educational establishments for the youngest children did not go away. The kindergarten movement had always taken children principally from the middle class, but there were instances of free or low-cost kindergartens in London and Salford, subsidized by profits from fee-paying settings or the donations of philanthropists. Some of those were taken over by local authorities after the Education Act of 1918 allowed them to use funds for pre-school education.

The term 'nursery education' began to be employed, although it was some time before it became standard. It emerged because Froebel's followers wanted to find an English equivalent to 'kindergarten'. There was a little embarrassment about being followers of a German thinker in the period just before the First World War when tensions between the UK and Germany were growing. In 1912 Miss Penstone, a leading figure in the National Froebel Union, thrilled the young radical teachers in her lecture audiences with her declaration that Froebel's contribution had been valuable, but he was 'too German'. She seems to have meant that he expected his approach to be applied too systematically and paid insufficient attention to what a later generation would call 'the unique child'. In the same year the first English translation of Maria Montessori's principal book on her approach was published. Quite quickly Montessori began to replace Froebel as the leading foreign theorist. This process was speeded by the First World War when Italy was Britain's ally against Germany.

So strong was Montessori's reputation that Margaret McMillan, who was the leading British figure in early childhood education after the War, displayed symptoms of real jealousy, claiming that it was she, not Montessori, who had first spotted the relevance of Séguin for the pedagogy in the early years.

The term 'nursery school' was used in 1890 by Mrs Michaelis of the Froebel Educational Institute. She may well have invented it. The most important event in the early twentieth century in the development of a British concept of education for the youngest children was Margaret McMillan's establishment of a nursery school in Deptford in London as part of a larger project for children she was conducting in the area. McMillan had been involved in Bradford's Board of Education between 1894 and 1902 and had been elected as a member of the Froebel Society's Executive in 1904 after she moved to London. In 1919 she published a book on nursery schools that ran through several editions up until her death (McMillan, 1930). The book was a best-seller and helped to establish her reputation as an original thinker in the field of early education, although Mary Chignell, who worked at Deptford between 1917 and 1920, claimed that much that was original about practice there had been due to her rather than McMillan (Steedman, 1990: 227).

Whatever McMillan's precise contribution to pedagogical theory and practice may have been, she was certainly effective as a publicist. Support grew for the idea of nursery schools – settings separate from elementary schools in which a proper education of children under 5 could operate. (Like many others, McMillan would have preferred nursery schools to cater for children aged 3–7, but she decided not to spend too much time banging her head against the brick wall of political and official support for the established law.) Manchester City Council had already opened two nursery schools in Ardwick and Collyhurst in 1915. In 1920 this was followed by the opening of a 'demonstration' nursery school under the aegis of Mather Training College, which was itself under the city's Education Committee. This school was intended to be a model that could be followed by others (Wood, 1934: 20, 55).

Such initiatives were stifled by the economic crisis that followed the First World War. In 1921 the Board of Education required local authorities to avoid any new expenditure in elementary education and it was provision for the under-5s that was usually held back. Similar things happened in the following year when Geddes, the Chancellor of the Exchequer, wielded his 'axe' on public services. In 1923 Grace Owen set up the Nursery Schools Association (NSA) to campaign for stronger commitment to separate pre-school education. In 1929 the new Labour Government (whose leader Ramsay MacDonald was a Vice-President of the NSA) promised expansion it never managed to achieve because of the escalating financial crisis and its own political defeat. A new round of public expenditure cuts in 1931 killed off any hope of real expansion for the time being.

Local authorities that wanted to see some growth in nursery education opted for nursery classes within elementary schools. Leicester was the leading example. This was a solution that was cheaper, but less likely to facilitate focus on the specific educational and other needs of younger children. Sometimes local authorities appear to have had considerations other than costs in mind. In 1933 Lilycroft Nursery School in Bradford was merged with the local infant school and Miriam Lord, the head of the nursery school, was demoted to the rank of an assistant. She had clashed with the local authority by publicly contesting its decisions on milk in school, had run parenting classes for fathers (as well as those for mothers) and had taught young girls what she called 'the elements of sexual hygiene' and all these things probably contributed to the decision to bring her under the control of the head of the local elementary school. The fact that she was instructed to stop her parenting classes suggests as much. It is also important to remember that many in the teaching profession had deep reservations about nursery schools. Where they existed, they restricted the size of primary schools and, therefore, the resources those schools could attract or the career opportunities they offered. Teachers also resented the strong involvement of the medical profession in the nursery schools. A booklet published in 1929 by the National Union of Teachers accepts many of the lessons coming from the nursery schools, but argues that they can be applied effectively in ordinary schools. Two academics working on teacher training declared that 'In view of the existing infant school system it would . . . be wasteful and, indeed, absurd to set up *ab initio* a sufficient number of Nursery Schools to meet the needs of the infant population of this society' (Wheeler and Earl, 1939: 25).

In 1933 the report of the Consultative Committee on Infant and Nursery Schools chaired by Sir William Hadow spoke of nursery schools as a 'desirable adjunct' to standard schooling. The principal role the Committee saw for such settings was as an 'asylum' for children whose home environment was 'unsuitable'. A hundred years after Hill had argued that all children needed early education, it was being officially defined as a compensatory measure for the deprived.

The economic situation was never universally bleak in the 1930s and by the middle of the decade there were signs of improvement outside the old industrial areas of the North. A declining birth rate, caused in part by the Depression, made it easier for local authorities to consider using space in schools for the under-5s again. In the 1935 general election all three major parties called for more nursery education. A ten-year plan was devised and local authorities were invited to estimate need in their own areas. The focus was still on pre-school provision as a remedial measure. A Board of Education leaflet saw 'the physical and medical nurture of the debilitated child' as the 'primary object' of nursery education. The NSA made the case for nursery schools on similar grounds. Whatever the reason given by government for encouraging it, there was at least renewed support for nursery education. Early years teachers were optimistic about the outlook. Cusden's 1938 book *The*

English Nursery School was typical in assuming that a period of large-scale expansion was about to start.

Day care and the origins of nursery nursing

By the early twentieth century infant and elementary schools were providing a day care as well as an educational service. The political establishment was never entirely comfortable with this and was only prepared to look favourably upon it when the financial situation looked reasonably secure. At the same time, settings specifically designed to have a day care function were rare.

It is interesting to compare the situation here with that of France, another industrially developed nation. In that country a philanthropist called Marbeau who had established day care settings for children under 2 whose mothers were at work or were otherwise unable to provide daytime care, had argued the case for them in a book he published in 1845 and launched a national network of what he called *crèches* that secured government endorsement later in the century.

Things were different in this country. It became common in Britain to denounce the employment of mothers as disastrous for their children. The evidence as to whether there was any justification for this is sparse. Most women who worked outside their homes were not the mothers of young children. It is, therefore, difficult to accept that their employment explains the fact that infant mortality continued to rise at a time when life expectancy for adults was improving. The limited capacity of the medical profession to deal adequately with fairly common life-threatening conditions and the appalling nature of much of the urban environment provide better explanations.

There were, however, some reasons for thinking that the employment of mothers was dangerous for their babies. No adequate substitutes for breast milk were available and this became a greater difficulty as the gulf between home and workplace widened and fewer employers were prepared to make provision for employees to breastfeed at work. The first formula for artificial food was introduced to Britain from Germany in 1867, but was expensive. It was not until Cow & Gate invented their roller-dried process in 1903 that a reasonably priced and healthy substitute for breast milk became widely available. Before that time relatives or neighbours caring for other people's children were likely to resort to one of the 'infant quietners' on the market, all of which were essentially low doses of opium suspended in syrup and certain to harm the children's health, often fatally. There is one piece of impressive evidence of the danger to babies of having mothers in the factories. The infant mortality rate declined significantly in Lancashire during the 'cotton famine' of 1862–64 (caused by the American Civil War) when many female employees were made redundant.

On the other hand, there is also evidence that high infant mortality had more significant causes than the employment of mothers. An investigation of social conditions in the Manchester district of Ancoats in the 1860s produced no evidence at all that the homes of female cotton operatives were worse kept than those of others in the neighbourhood (Hewitt, 1958: 74). One key piece of evidence came from Dr Bland, the first Medical Officer of Health for Macclesfield where an unusually large number of women were working in the textile industry. In his first annual report in 1873, Bland pointed out that areas of low female employment, such as Liverpool, had high rates of infant mortality. He also reported that a detailed survey he had conducted demonstrated that infant mortality rates were *lower* in the districts of Macclesfield that had high rates of female employment than they were in other districts (Garwood, 1988). Bland brought a sharply critical mind to a controversy that was usually conducted on the basis of sweeping assumptions. It was a minor disaster that his own ill health (possibly brought on by his attention to duty) led to his early retirement in 1885.

His colleagues rarely followed him in his careful attention to the facts. In 1874 the Medical Officer of Health for Bolton asserted that the high infant mortality rate in the town could be blamed squarely on the employment of women in factories. He called for a national system of 'infant nurseries' to solve the problem. However, he assumed that these would have to be financed from fees paid by parents. He did not explain how he thought low-waged factory employees would afford this or take into consideration what had happened earlier to unsubsidized day care (Horn, 1997: 58).

Day nurseries opened in the mid-century had rarely survived for long. A few initiatives in the last three decades of the nineteenth century demonstrated what might be possible, especially when employers wanted to assist their own employees. Courtaulds, the major employer in Halstead, opened a workplace nursery to replace the failed venture of Mrs Clements. Nurseries subsidized by cotton manufacturers opened in Manchester, Salford and Eccles. There were similar projects in Leicester and at Enderley Mills in Newcastle-under-Lyne. Sometimes the connections between nursery provision and employers were a little less direct. In 1873 a group of ladies in Sheffield (all of them from families owning major steel factories where women were often employed in less skilled work) decided to open a day nursery for working mothers. The setting was intended for mothers who were 'obliged to go out to work', usually because they were widows, but the service was later opened up to the offspring of women unfortunate enough to have 'dissolute and drunken husbands' (Mercer, 1996: 276–7). The nursery was still in operation as a children's centre at the beginning of the twenty-first century.

Many settings that were launched in the second half of the nineteenth century and were not attached to specific workplaces ran into financial difficulty because they failed to attract sufficient custom. The fees they charged must have discouraged some from using them. It also seems that many parents preferred to make use of childminders in their own neighbourhoods, partly because they did not want to 'take bread out of the mouths' of those women, partly because they resented having to demonstrate respectability to secure nursery places (Hewitt, 1958: 165–6).

Alarm about the high rate of infant mortality did more to promote day care than concern for working mothers. McMillan's first nursery school in Deptford grew out of what was essentially a health promotion project. Other day care projects had similar origins. For example, the City of Westminster Health Society started a day nursery in 1927 as part of its programme of health promotion. The Society's annual report for 1930/1 listed the grounds for admission as 'nervousness, lack of sleep and appetite caused by want of fresh air, convalescence and general delicacy, precocity or want of discipline'.

In spite of the concerns about health and the need to bring more women into the factories during the First World War, the expansion that might have been expected in the first half of the twentieth century faded away. There were 174 nurseries in England and Wales in 1919, but 70 fewer by 1938 (Halloran, 1982: 22). Where there was any expansion, it was in nursery classes or in the residential nurseries run by voluntary organizations, such as National Children's Homes and Barnardo's.

The agencies running residential nurseries were interested in securing training for their staff. There were fewer attempts to provide training for employees in day care. The foundations of professional nursery nursing had less to do with such services than they did with meeting the demands of the middle classes for servants properly trained in childcare. In 1892 Emily Ward opened the first training college for nannies and people in similar positions – the Norland Institute. So successful was this venture that for many decades people referred to a qualified nanny as a 'norland' wherever she had been trained (just as all vacuum cleaners came to be called 'hoovers').

When *Nursery World* started publication in 1925 it advertised itself as a journal for mothers and nurses and felt it could claim in the first editorial: 'The bad old days when every woman was supposed to know by instinct how to nurse, feed and teach children have gone forever: the art of looking after children is recognized as an art if not a science.' Nursery nursing may have been recognized by then as an art. It was still seen as requiring only modest skill. Mrs Ward had envisaged that her students would be 'well brought-up and educated girls who had neither the desire nor the scholarship to pass examinations' but wanted a career (*Nursery World*, 1925).

Nevertheless, moves towards better professional training progressed. In 1906 a national association for day nurseries was launched in an effort to raise standards. The idea of having an association of nursery training colleges was floated in 1913. It met with some approval from the relevant bodies, but was shelved when war broke out the following year. In 1920 the National Society of Day Nurseries pioneered a training programme for the staff of its affiliates. A number of local authorities, including Manchester, set up training schemes for 'nursery helpers', that is to say, girls who had left school at 14 and were waiting to start training as hospital nurses when they reached 18. In 1925 an Association of Nursery Training Colleges was launched and this was followed by the creation of a professional body, the Nursery Nurses Association. In 1932 the Royal Sanitary Institute (the principal body at the time for the training and education of medical nurses) started examinations for nursery nurses in London and Liverpool. Seven years later the nursery nursing profession joined the Whiteley Council system in which negotiations over the pay and conditions for medical nurses took place.

The last two developments marked an association between medical and nursery nursing that lasted long enough for the official guidance on Part X of the 1989 Children Act to describe medical nursing qualifications as suitable for those in charge of registered early childhood settings (Department of Health, 1991).

By 1939 important steps had been taken towards the creation of a profession of nursery nursing, but the foundations had also been laid for many of the difficulties that dogged that profession in the last part of the twentieth century.

Baby farming and childminding

In 1641 a case came before York quarter sessions concerning an illegitimate child whose father had it 'put to nurse' with someone who failed to care for the child properly once the father stopped payments until it was 'ready to starve for want of necessarys' (Pinchbeck and Hewitt, 1969: 218). The court was in something of a dilemma as there were no clear guidelines as to where responsibility for the child's welfare lay. Cases similar to that in York probably arose over the next couple of centuries, but the issue only became one of public debate in the 1860s.

By that time the old 'dame schools' were going out of existence. Their educational function was now met by the infant schools. Their childminding function was taken up usually by local women well known to the working mothers who employed them, but sometimes by people known as 'baby farmers' who operated on a more commercial scale and might foster children for weeks at a time or provide a kind of informal adoption service. In 1862 Ellen Barlee, a religious author with an interest in the conditions of the poor, found a large number of women providing childminding services in Lancashire (Barlee, 1863). Thirty years later when Mrs Ashworth from Burnley conducted a survey of working mothers, she found that half of their children were left in the care of neighbours who charged for this service (Perkin, 1993: 192–3).

In 1868 an inquest took place in London on the death of a baby that had died from hypothermia when the woman caring for him became incapacitated with drink. This was one of several cases that led a journalist called Greenwood to include a chapter on 'baby farming' in his sensational book *The Seven Curses of London* (1869). Incompetence and drunkenness were not the only issues. Baby farmers were often paid a one-off fee for long-term fostering. It was easier and cheaper for them to allow their charges to die from neglect than to care for the children properly. Greenwood believed that fathers of illegitimate children positively encouraged baby farmers to do this.

The law was not really equipped to tackle the issue. Mary Hall, a baby farmer from Camberwell in London, probably murdered some of the children in her care, but the prosecution despaired of trying to prove it and instead went for a charge of fraud. Other baby farmers were less lucky. Margaret Waters was hanged for murder soon after Greenwood's book was published. The willingness of the jury to convict may have had something to do with the impact of his call for action. The most notorious case came in 1896 when Amelia Dyer was hanged for killing children she had fostered. The evidence suggests she murdered many more children than those that featured in her trial, perhaps over three hundred of them.

A campaign organization called the Infant Life Protection Society demanded regulation of all people who cared for children under 6 years of age outside the children's own homes. Greenwood had proposed this in his book. There were vociferous protests from those who saw this as unwarranted interference in the private lives of families and the homes of those who minded children on a daily basis. The Infant Life Protection Act that was passed in 1872 required the registration and inspection only of those who cared for two or more children in their first year of life for longer than 24 hours at a time. After the Dyer case, the Act was amended to cover all children under 5 years of age and to place clearer responsibilities on Medical Officers of Health for registration and inspection. It remained a fairly feeble piece of legislation. It may have done something to inhibit the worst baby farmers and it proved useful during the two world wars in providing registers of childminders for working mothers to contact. It did not achieve much more in terms of day care, although it laid the foundation for later child protection legislation and the regulation of fostering and adoption.

Was there really a difference between baby farming and childminding in the late nineteenth century?

It became common in the second half of the twentieth century to suggest that there had been a clear distinction in the late nineteenth century between baby farmers and those women minding on a daily basis who offered a service which, if not positively approved, was, as Owen (1989) puts it, 'unobjectionable' and considered too private a matter to warrant intervention by the state. The reality was probably more complex. As well as the handful of baby farmers whose murderous activities are a matter of record, it is customary to refer to Mrs Squires, the wicked baby farmer in Moore's 1894 novel *Esther Walters*, who hints that she would be willing to allow Esther's illegitimate child to die of neglect in her care for a suitable fee. It is often forgotten that Mrs Squires is a daily childminder as well as someone offering long-term fostering. It is also often forgotten that there is another baby farmer in the novel – Mrs Lewis – whose generous support to Esther makes possible the novel's happy ending. The shadows of Mrs Dyer and Mrs Squires were to haunt childminding for some time to come. As a result those who want to defend childminding have dismissed those two as 'baby farmers' rather than proper childminders in a way that suggests a clearer distinction than existed in the 1890s.

Greenwood and others raised a real issue, but they were also part of a backlash against the idea of children being cared for by women other than their mothers. In France at the same time there was a similar moral panic about what had been the widespread practice of 'wet-nursing', that is to say, giving babies to women other than their mothers to breastfeed. It was widely suggested that this was the principal cause of the spread of syphilis in the homes of the affluent – something for which more plausible explanations were readily available.

Play

In a sermon preached in Sheffield in 1874, the Rev. James Russell spoke lyrically of the 'blessing' of children playing in the street. He saw this as evidence that they were in good health, felt safe in their neighbourhood and got on well together. His response to children's play may surprise those who see the Victorians as irredeemably gloomy, but it was typical of one strand of public opinion. In the second half of the century there was a new emphasis on the need to provide outdoor space for recreation in the towns and cities. A Recreation Ground Act was passed in 1859. Local authorities built playgrounds for children. Manchester had 16 of them by 1896, half a dozen with on-the-spot staff (Hanley, 1981). They appear to have been intended mainly for school-age children, as were the 'evening play centres' set up during the First World War in Sheffield to facilitate their mothers' employment (Keeble Hawson, 1968). Nevertheless, the basis for the twentieth-century profession of playwork was being laid.

There was also a potential impact on services for the youngest children. The central place of the garden in McMillan's model of the nursery school had its origins in her experience of running 'outdoor camps' for older children in

Deptford. After the First World War the assumption that children would feel safe to play on the streets was undermined by the motorcar. The relatively small number of cars actually contributed to the hazard since neither drivers nor child pedestrians were used to coping with each other. *Nursery World* recognized the problem and spoke of the importance of play centres in 1936. During the Second World War play centres were at first closed because of the risk from bombs, but they soon re-opened to meet demand and new ideas began to emerge on how they could be used. A book by Marie Paneth published in 1944 offered a theoretical basis for a less supervisory and more facilitating approach to their management.

Mother and child services and 'mothercraft'

The problem of infant mortality offered the most acceptable argument for day care for young children. The question was whether another strategy might work better. Some people recognized that where parental behaviour and not problems of bad food, housing and sanitation could be held responsible for children's deaths, it was often ignorance rather than negligence that was to blame. It took decades for scientific advances in the understanding of how food became contaminated to reach the wider public.

A VOICE FROM THE TIME

The need to educate mothers

Now we have only to look around us to see innumerable instances in which the child's health and even life falls a sacrifice to uneducated maternal instinct, displaying itself in the administration of improper food, clothing or curative experiments. The maternal instinct must be elevated into the realm of conscious intelligence before it can act with security for the infant.

Source: (Baroness von Marenholtz-Bülow, 1855: 11)

This passage is taken from something written in the middle of the nineteenth century. It would be possible to find similar opinions expressed from the beginning of that century to the present day. Interestingly, this is a relatively modern phenomenon. It is difficult to find similar views expressed before 1800.

The solution to inadequate parenting was seen by some to lie in new supportive and instructional services. The Manchester and Salford Ladies Sanitary Reform

Association (often regarded as the origin of health visiting) had been launched in 1862. By the end of the nineteenth century several local authorities had appointed 'lady health missionaries' and 'travelling teachers of hygiene'. School medical services, which had begun in the 1890s (for example, in Bradford where Margaret McMillan did much to launch the system), were given legislative underpinning. Midwifery, which had been largely outside the control of doctors, became more strictly regulated. The loss of life during the First World War heightened anxieties about breeding a new generation of soldiers. A Save The Babies Week was organized in 1917. Voluntary organizations, such as the Provident Maternity Club in St. Pancras in London, argued for more activity by local authorities. In 1918 a comprehensive Maternity and Child Welfare Act, building on earlier legislation in 1915, created new services for recently born children and their mothers. This was supplemented later by the appointment of 'houseworkers' or 'home helps' to provide assistance to mothers at about the time of confinement. It was the fact that the Boer War and the First World War had done so much to encourage efforts to preserve the nation's children that led Dwork to give her 1987 history of maternity and child welfare services the deliberately disconcerting title *War is Good for Babies and Other Children*.

Not everyone was happy about this. In the 1920s the Mothers Defence League opposed all forms of statutory intervention in family life (Lewis, 1984: 39). Other lobbyists argued that the education of current and future mothers would ensure that families would not need support in the longer term. Some of this work could be undertaken in schools. 'Domestic economy' became a compulsory subject for girls in the elementary schools. Outside the school system Henriette Schrader-Breymann, a leading member of the Froebel movement, encouraged her English followers to establish a 'House for Home and Life Training' in London, offering both an individual casework service and formal classes.

In 1903 Elizabeth Sloane Chesser published an influential book on the need to train mothers in the interests of the nation. Mabel Liddiard's *Mothercraft Manual*, first published in 1924, was even more successful. It went through numerous editions and was still determining attitudes in the 1950s. Liddiard emphasized routine and discipline in the raising of small children. Her preferred method for dealing with children who persisted in sucking their thumbs or playing with their genitals was to semi-immobilize them with carefully applied splints. She and her principal mentor Dr Truby-King believed that anything but the most rigid structuring of a child's life would lead to physical and moral degeneration. Thanks to them it became established practice to prevent contact between mothers and their children in hospitals and residential care in case this led to emotional disturbance. The two of them inflicted massive harm, not only at the time they were influential, but also in the 1960s when a backlash led many to the dangerous conclusion that to create any kind of structure for a young child's life was to be oppressive.

Teaching mothers how to do their job properly became an established part of many health and other services for young children. From 1913 and for many years after that, the City of Westminster Health Society, one of the pioneers in the field, ran 'mothercraft classes' at which local women practised sewing while listening to lectures on various aspects of child-rearing. It was generally agreed that services of this kind were needed. There was less clarity on what should go into them. A Mothercraft Training Society was established, but did not have a secure base of its own until 1943. By that time the idea was more widely accepted. Major Nathan, Chairman of the National Society of Children's Nurseries, argued not only for a comprehensive system of nurseries after the war, but also for attaching 'mothercraft centres' to them (Nathan, 1943). In other words, he envisaged something like the centres set up later under the Sure Start programme. None of his proposals came to anything immediately after the Second World War, but the notion of a service that supported parents directly as well as by providing day care was already around.

The Second World War

There was widespread anxiety in the period leading up to and shortly after the start of the war about what aerial bombardment might do to the civilian population, in particular to children. This was fed by knowledge of what had happened to the town of Guernica during the Spanish Civil War and by the graphic depiction of bombing at the start of the film *The Shape of Things to Come*. A rushed evacuation took place in September 1939, although nearly 90 per cent of evacuated children were back at home by the beginning of 1940. The government was not prepared at that time to consider proposals for nursery centres and workplace nurseries, believing they would be too expensive and would make the children in them vulnerable to enemy bombing raids (Minns, 1980).

One consequence of this is that nursery schools and classes played a greater role in releasing mothers for paid employment during the war than is often recognized. Where day care for working mothers was advocated, officials expressed preference for schemes that mirrored the kind of arrangements working-class women often made for themselves. They cost less and were seen as less disruptive to family life. The 'volunteer housewife scheme' was entirely informal, unsupervised and unpaid. A more formalized scheme was that of the so-called 'guardians', childminders whose services to mothers were subsidized by the state and who were regulated by local health officials. The degree of oversight entailed proved to be too intrusive for many. In Sheffield only one person ever registered under the scheme and there was a similar response elsewhere (Stanniland, 1989: 50–2). The demand for more nursery places (including residential nurseries) to be provided increased.

This was always controversial and health officials usually saw the provision of day care as an unfortunate necessity that could be abandoned once the war was over. Views hostile to nurseries were expressed at the 1943 Conference of the National Baby Welfare Council. Some even questioned whether the provision of nurseries on a large scale really helped the war effort. Hughes (1942) suggested that it would be better to pay mothers of young children to stay at home and thereby release nursery workers for the munitions factories. Her assertion was that, because nursery care was labour-intensive, almost as many women would be employed in undertaking it as were released for other 'war work'. I am not aware of any research to examine whether this calculation was reasonable. In terms of sheer numbers alone it sounds plausible. Hughes's argument does not, however, take issues of age, skills and personal wishes into account.

The fact is that the demand for nurseries had many sources besides the wish to supplement the workforce and boost war-time production, especially of armaments. It had long been true that many women who accepted the traditional roles of wife and mother were, nevertheless, forced to work because their husbands were dead or missing or rendered incapable by accident or disease of doing the sort of jobs that paid well. The number of women in such situations naturally increased during the war when men in the armed forces became casualties of enemy action. This was also the first time in British history since the seventeenth century that large numbers of civilians were caught up directly in armed conflict. Some women developed a new view of themselves. Left-wing women's organizations encouraged this, pointing to the gender equality they alleged was enjoyed in the Soviet Union.

Work with young children also offered a suitably 'feminine' career for young women. This appealed to many of them, creating the basis for a new interest in nursery nursing as a career. At the end of 1943 a Nursery Nurses' Guild was launched in Birmingham, an unsuccessful attempt to have a more assertive alternative to the NNA. By the autumn of 1944, more than 106,000 children under 5 were in recognized day care (Minns, 1980: 26–9) and this figure does not take into account a large number of childminders, play centres, extended nursery class hours and other arrangements. The editor of *Nursery World* did not want to see the new nurseries kept open after the end of the war in Europe, but published several contributions on the journal's letter pages from women who took the opposite view. The defenders of early childhood services assumed that things would be much better than before when peace came.

Conclusion

The period 1870–1945 saw

- the establishment of a state system of elementary schooling which had many positive effects, but also the severe drawback of requiring formal education to start at around the time of the child's fifth birthday;

- support (growing out of the kindergarten movement and McMillan's work in Deptford) for nursery education as a distinct type of provision;
- the development of day care services and the first very tentative attempts to take childminding out of the private into the public sphere;
- a new concern about children's health and the ways young mothers should be supported;
- the beginnings of playwork as an area of provision.

This was a great deal. Development was incomplete and always vulnerable to cuts at times of economic crisis, but there were grounds for optimism about the future of early childhood services in 1945.

Exercise

Try to find a copy of Margaret McMillan's *The Nursery School*. It may not be on the shelves of your college or university library or the largest public library in your area, but, if you ask, you may well find it is kept in some kind of store. How familiar do the ideas and attitudes in that book seem to you today? What is less familiar?

Further reading

Steedman's biography of Margaret McMillan (1990) is a particularly useful account of her life and the background to it.

Brehony's (2000) article on 'The Kindergarten in England 1851–1918' is as interesting on the period after 1870 as for the twenty years beforehand.

Dwork's (1987) book *War is Good for Babies and Other Children* is a good account of the early days of maternity and child welfare services.

Whitbread's (1972) history of the nursery-infant school was published some time ago, but is still relevant.

Pugh's *State and Society* (2008) describes the social and political history of the period covered in this chapter. Clarke's *Hope and Glory* (2004) is good on the period after 1900.

There is now a growing body of literature on women's history. Perkin's *Victorian Women* (1993) is a good introduction to the earlier part of the period covered in this chapter. Hewitt's *Wives and Mothers in Victorian Industry* was published as long ago as 1958, but still offers the best coverage of the subject.

3 Early childhood services in the period of post-war consensus (1945–1979)

After the Second World War there was considerable agreement about the value of the welfare state. However, services for young children failed to become a central feature of social policy and, just when it seemed that their status might be enhanced, the welfare state itself was thrown into question.

This chapter describes:

- how the pre-war expectation that early childhood services would soon enjoy a period of expansion were disappointed;
- how the end of the 1960s saw renewed hopes for such an expansion;
- how these hopes were threatened – in spite of a new wave of feminism – by the financial and other crises of the 1970s.

The Labour Government of 1945 and the creation of the welfare state

A general election was held in 1945. The Labour Party won and was expected to introduce large-scale reforms in social policy, in a phrase that came into common use, to replace the warfare state with a welfare state. Their reforms were both popular and far-reaching. At the same time they were not as revolutionary as many had hoped or feared. It was not a socialist transformation for which the electorate had voted but better health care, greater financial security, modern kitchens for housewives and less need for people to be deferential to their social superiors. There were important differences of detail, but the social policy programme the Labour Party put forward did not differ fundamentally from the one proposed by the leading Conservative Harold Macmillan in 1938 and which he later put into operation as minister of housing and then prime minister.

Early childhood services in the New Welfare State

Nursery schools and nurseries failed to secure a central position in Atlee's welfare state, in spite of the hopes there had been before and during the war. It has often been asserted – by me among others – that the government created childcare places when the war started because it needed women to work in the factories and then got rid of those places quickly once the war was over, forcing women back to the home. This is an over-simplification. In an unpublished dissertation that deals with events in Sheffield during the war and immediately afterwards, Stanniland (1989) describes the complexity of what actually happened. Once the war had started, the government was initially reluctant to accept that day care might be important to production. The pressure for better day care did not come from the government at first, but from the NSA and other professional bodies, working women, many industrialists and the political left. That support had been there before 1939 and was as important as the production priorities in securing change.

Women's employment continued to rise after the war and in 1947 there was a production drive during which women were encouraged back to work. While the number of places in day nurseries declined quite drastically soon after the end of the war, other forms of daytime care continued to be available and there were places (including Sheffield) where cuts in nursery provision took place much later.

It is, of course, true that there was a demand that mothers return to the home. War-time nurseries had been, in the words of one correspondent to *Nursery World* (issue of 10/5/45), 'painful necessities' and not 'the ideal life for the baby'. When Beveridge wrote his famous 1942 report that provided the basis for the new welfare state, he assumed that everything would be done to encourage mothers to stay at home to ensure the viability of Britain. He shared the fears of many that the population was going into numerical decline and the empire would suffer accordingly. In 1945 (after the 'baby boom' had started) the Ministry of Health in an often-quoted passage said that its policy was to 'positively discourage mothers of children under two from going to work'. In 1946 day nurseries were made the financial responsibility of local authorities at a time when they had less money to spend. The decline in the number of less skilled jobs in the early 1950s, the return of men who had been in the armed forces in the Far East and – in some places – the recruitment of immigrant workers from the Caribbean and elsewhere led to nursery closures across the country as fewer women were 'needed'. Nine out of 17 day nurseries closed in Sheffield in 1953 (Stanniland, 1989: 82).

Back to normality (with improvements)

When there were reductions in childcare places, some people objected, others did not. No doubt, many women had gained new confidence from their experience of 'war work' and took pride in their contribution to the war effort. This was not true of all of them. A report by Mass Observation found exactly the opposite in a factory staffed almost entirely by women working on radar equipment. Most saw their jobs as a boring necessity (Harrison, 1943). After the war material conditions were appallingly drab, if not actually grim. What people wanted was a version of the improving social and economic situation of the late 1930s, an escape from austerity into the world of the Ideal Home Exhibition.

The longing for normality resulted in the age at which people married dropping drastically. It reached an all-time low for the modern era, staying that way until the early 1970s. Many moved from the older working-class neighbourhoods in the East End of London and elsewhere to new council housing estates, New Towns or (a little later) suburban owner-occupied developments. The dream of a radical separation of work and home was being achieved, but it was not always as much fun as had been anticipated. Even before the war there had been talk of 'suburban neurosis'. After the war the problem spread from the middle-class suburbs to new working-class communities. Research began in the 1950s and was widely reported in the early 1960s on what Taylor and Chave (1964) called 'sub-clinical neurosis' and the press dubbed 'new town blues'. The Institute for Community Studies examined how the solidarity of older working-class neighbourhoods (which had included informal childcare, although this was not something that greatly interested the male researchers) was being replaced by a more anonymous kind of existence (Young and Willmott, 1962).

Advances in the quality of food, medicine, water supplies and child welfare services meant that the health of young children was considerably better. The anxieties about babies that afflicted even middle-class housewives in the middle of the previous century (and were reflected in the famous book by Mrs Beeton, 1861: 1025–60) were assuaged. The growing availability of domestic machinery (cookers, washing machines, vacuum cleaners, etc.) reduced the amount of sheer grind in which many housewives had had to engage before the war. That must have been an enormous relief. The problem of the 'servantless household' had been much discussed in magazines with middle-class readers in the 1920s and 1930s. Now machines replaced the servants and started to become more widely available than servants had ever been. It is also possible that the Newsons (1965: 140) were correct to suggest that the absence of servants encouraged fathers to play a more active part in their young children's care after the war, taking some small part of the burden from mothers.

At the same time the reduction in the sheer quantity of work may have engendered a sense of emptiness for women who now had so much time at home and may have added to the financial motives for young mothers to seek paid work. New educational opportunities for working-class and lower middle-class children, although more accessible in practice to boys than to girls, opened up the prospect of more interesting careers just as automation was beginning to reduce the amount of less skilled work available in factories. It took a while for the discontent of many housewives to come to the surface, but it was growing.

The residual role of early childhood services

The argument that childcare was essential to the boosting of production seemed out of date to most politicians and officials by the 1950s. Day nurseries were seen as a service for families in difficulty and the origins of the problems those families suffered were often considered to lie with those families themselves. Homes that were physically unhealthy were being replaced in a programme of slum clearance. The problem that was now more widely identified was that of homes that were malfunctioning psychologically. Even those who advocated retaining some of the war-time nurseries did so on the grounds that such places were needed for mothers who had not learned childcare properly or found it difficult to cope with a new baby when the previous child was still young. Such people were bound to be in a minority. Nurseries might still be required, but only on a very restricted scale.

The regulation of childcare

The belief that day care had a residual, compensatory role showed itself, not just in massively reduced local authority provision, but in the introduction of closer regulation of the private sector. During the war public health officials had worried that hastily established nursery centres lacked proper facilities and might be a breeding ground for infections (Women's Group on Public Welfare, 1943). After the war they worried that, as state provision was reduced, inadequate private provision catering to irresponsible mothers would take its place. In 1948 an Act was passed, subjecting private and voluntary day nurseries to a new process of registration and inspection. MPs were as reluctant as their predecessors in 1871 to regulate childminding and thereby interfere with what was happening in people's homes. The experience with the wartime Guardians Scheme was discouraging. However, it was difficult to distinguish between private nurseries and childminders working with assistants. For this reason childminders were also covered by the 1948 Act. The Parliamentary Secretary to the Ministry of Health made it clear that it was those who treated childminding as a business who were the target of new regulation rather than childminders assisting neighbours, even when they did so for money (Owen, 2006: 25). The 1948 Act marked a crucial turning point. Regulation was to remain the primary intervention by central government in children's day care for more than fifty years.

Nursery nursing and the NNEB

The other reflection of the restricted and low status of day nurseries was what happened to nursery nursing. A National Association of Certificated Nursery Nurses was launched in 1948 (the latest in a series of not very successful efforts to create a professional body). From the foundation of the Norland Institute there had been attempts to create a proper system of training for nursery nurses. A National Nurseries Examination Board (NNEB) was set up for England and Wales in 1945 and a similar body in Scotland the following year (Wright, 1999). In the absence of any real drive from central government for a system of day nurseries, the creation of the NNEB could do little for the professional status for nursery nurses. Students usually began courses at a young age. (Some courses were actually conducted in secondary schools.) The training they received was not designed to equip them for much in the way of independent judgement.

When it started, the NNEB was closely connected with and subordinate to the relevant bodies for professional training in medical nursing. This reflected the domination of day care by health services during the war. Hilda Cunnington, who was appointed in 1943 to be the 'educational supervisor' in Sheffield's nurseries, found there was 'no education to supervise' and the emphasis was totally on physical care (Briggs, 1978: 78). A colleague, Miss Jolly, who was responsible for training women who joined the war-time Child Care Reserve, found her ideas on play blocked by matrons and other nursery staff who considered such activity incompatible with hygiene (Briggs, 1978: 80–5). In 1947 the two of them set up the first course in the city leading to the NNEB qualification. Cunnington was convinced by her war-time experience that there was no future in local authority nurseries and encouraged her students to prepare for work as nannies. Someone who took her course remembers a constant emphasis on deportment and etiquette (essential for acceptance in middle-class homes at the time) and that she could – without any trace of irony – describe the course as 'a finishing school for the daughters of the respectable working class'.

Nursery schools

If day nurseries fell in status as well as numbers, nursery schools fared no better. The expansion in nursery education that was anticipated in 1938/39 never happened. In 1945 the Ministry of Education had argued that nursery schools had a broad educational purpose and were not there just to compensate for inadequate family homes. Two years later the Minister of Education said 'The present situation does not allow us to go ahead with such projects as nursery schools and community centres. They are desirable, but in the present circumstances they cannot be allowed to take up labour and materials' (*Nursery World*, 13/11/47: 1273). It was neither the first nor the last time that financial restraint was given as the reason for cutting back on early childhood services. The Nursery Schools Association, which had been optimistic and assertive during the war, began to back down and to defend nursery education in terms of their compensatory function, making them a special service for the deprived in much the same way (though with better qualified staff) as the day nurseries were.

Playwork and the adventure playground

The one area of growth and innovation in services for young children was that of playwork. The world's first adventure playground (built in Denmark in 1943) was not well known in Britain at the time as Denmark was under German occupation. However, after the war, Lady Allen of Hartwood had a chance encounter with the project at Emdrupvaenge and was inspired by it. In 1946 she wrote about it enthusiastically in the popular magazine *Picture Post*. Bombing raids had left plenty of derelict sites in London and the major industrial cities. This provided an excellent opportunity to create new play spaces for children. Residents who did not want the quiet and tidiness of their streets disturbed objected vociferously. The British invented the term 'adventure playground' because the literal translation of the original Danish phrase 'junk playground' aroused suspicion. Lady Allen persisted and gathered support. New opportunities for outdoor play were, after all, essential because of increased motor traffic, the housing of more and more families in tower blocks and the determination of council housing official to keep their estates neat and presentable rather than places where children could play.

A few adventure playgrounds were opened in London. In 1953 the National Playing Fields Association established its Playground Committee, which was joined in 1956 by Drummond Abernathy who was later to open the first playwork course in the UK at Thurrock. The movement was spread by the enthusiastic activity and the writings of Joe Benjamin (1974). That initial expansion shuddered to a near halt by the end of the 1970s, but the adventure playground movement had created a base for professional play leadership of the sort suggested during the war by Paneth.

Changes in family life in the 1960s

As the country began to emerge from austerity, changes in family life had consequences for the way in which early years services were seen.

A book on childcare by the American Dr Spock had had a popular following in the United States since its publication there in 1946. It appeared in Britain (with a new title) in 1958 and had a tremendous impact, encouraging parents to enter into more spontaneous relationships with their children and ending the long reign of Mabel Liddiard (see Chapter 2, p. 41). *Nursery World*, whose principal readers had been nannies and nursery nurses, began to describe itself as the magazine for 'the modern mother', the woman who did not quarrel with her task, but wanted ideas on how to undertake it properly. Changing attitudes were recorded meticulously and sympathetically by John and Elizabeth Newson (1965, 1968) on the basis of surveys they conducted among parents of young children in Nottingham.

The renewed emphasis on affection between parents and children was excellent, but also had the potential to keep mothers tied to the home. Much has been made of the influence of Bowlby with his emphasis on the need of children to form and maintain close attachments to certain adults. Most of his original research had been conducted on children whose lives had been disrupted very severely and had suffered as a result. He never denied – as some admirers and detractors claimed he did – that children should begin from an early age to build up relationships outside the nuclear family or that adults other than biological mothers could play the key role in bringing up their children. Bowlby came to be blamed for the lack of childcare in the 1950s and 1960s (something caused by greater factors than his limited influence). It was hard luck for him – or at least for his later reputation – that he published a popular version of his ideas in 1963, long after the research on which they were based. This was just in time to influence concepts of children's needs in the local authority children's departments and, as a result, to attract the enmity of the feminist movement that began to emerge at the end of the 1960s.

Interest in the welfare of children brought new problems to the fore. As early as 1962 *Nursery World* warned that the availability of new and cheaper food might lead to childhood obesity, an issue taken up later in the decade by Dr Cross (1969). The abuse of children, especially abuse by their parents, was another problem that received greater publicity. Local authority children's departments had been launched in 1948 in response to the scandal caused by the killing of a child by his new foster parents. Three years earlier the nation had been shocked by a case of serious child abuse in Wallasey. In spite of this, child protection was not highlighted in the way it might have been until the end of the 1960s when the term 'battered baby syndrome' was devised. Matters came to a head in the next decade with the case of Maria Colwell, a girl killed by her stepfather in spite of the support being offered the family by a local authority social workers. After that child protection began to take centre stage in social work and to become critically important in other professions such as nursery nursing, health visiting and teaching.

At the same time further changes were taking place in attitudes to the family home. The importation of the American invention of 'babysitting' represented a modest, but indicative modification of the boundaries between the family home and the outside world (Best, 1962). Yudkin and Holme (1963) in their survey of working mothers were more sympathetic than earlier commentators had been and highlighted the difficulties caused by lack of day care.

The rediscovery of poverty

The welfare state was assumed in 1950 to have brought an end to poverty. In the 1960s, following similar developments in the United States, a 'rediscovery' of poverty took place among social researchers. Abel-Smith and Townsend (1965) wrote the best-known text, but there were many others. It appeared that poverty was, after all, not confined to a small number of 'problem families' who were unable for reasons psychoanalysts might best explain to take advantage of economic prosperity and the welfare state. It had a structural dimension. Poverty – and what to do about it – were back on the political agenda. It is difficult now after several decades of debate about welfare dependency to appreciate how shocking this was in the 1960s. 'Isn't it terrible that we should be talking about the poor again?' an older colleague asked me in 1967 with obvious anguish. The idea that early childhood services might have an important part to play in solving the problem of poverty became significant in the following decade.

Immigration

Another social change that was beginning to affect early childhood services was that brought about by immigration from the Commonwealth that had started at the end of the 1940s. The arrival of many people (usually young and, therefore bringing children with them or having them here once they had begun to settle), people who differed from the majority in their physical appearance and customs, was a visible sign of social and political change and especially of the end of empire. It rattled people and some of the responses were angry, even violent.

This situation was not completely new for those working in early childhood services. Back in the 1920s the City of Westminster Health Society had published leaflets on maternity and child welfare in Yiddish and Italian as part of its effort to meet the needs of two of the principal immigrant communities in central London. By the end of the 1960s some settings were doing their best to respond to new needs. In June 1966 the *Manchester Evening News* carried an article describing the work of Hilary Keays, a 17-year-old volunteer, who had set up a playgroup catering for children of Pakistani origin in the city. Another pioneering venture was the David Gretton Nursery in Birmingham, which made a particular effort to reach out to families of South Asian origin (Elias, 1969). It took some time, however, for the great majority of services dealing with young children to appreciate that all of them – not just those in the minority of urban neighbourhoods where many black and Asian people were to be found – would have to respond to the new multicultural society that was emerging.

The formation of the Pre-School Playgroups Association

In general, those who recognized that social changes implied the need for different early childhood services were young, often surprisingly young. It may seem extraordinary that the person who set up the project in Manchester just mentioned should have been only 17. It was in some ways typical. In the early 1970s an organization called the Young Christian Students, consisting of older school pupils and some students in further and higher education, launched many of the first community playschemes in various parts of England. The principal achievement in the early years field in the period also came from outside the mainstream. In 1960 Belle Tutaev, a young mother, got together with people she had met through the Register of Housebound Housewives to set up their own nursery in the absence of any local authority provision in the part of London in which they lived. The following year she sent a letter about it to the *Guardian*. The response was colossal and led to the launch of a Nursery Schools Campaign. In 1962 the organization had its first annual general meeting. By that time it had become the National Association of Pre-School Playgroups (later the Pre-School Playgroups Association – PPA – now the Pre-school Learning Alliance).

The organization was considerably more assertive in its demands for better provision than the Nursery Schools Association had been after the war. It transformed itself rapidly into a network of pre-school playgroups similar to the one Tutaev had started herself. This encouraged new ideas on the participation of parents, especially mothers, in the education of their children. The teaching profession had developed since the early part of the century in ways that led to the virtual exclusion of parents from active participation in their children's education. This was particularly true of nursery schools and classes, although this was far from being the intention of McMillan and others like her.

Parents were discouraged from trying to teach their children anything beyond basic self-care. Wynne had written in 1936 'school teachers infinitely prefer virgin soil to a little garden full of the weeds of faulty measures'. That attitude lasted well into the 1970s, but the PPA challenged it forcefully.

Tutaev was a teacher before she had children. She was typical of a change in the infant teaching profession. Up until the early 1960s many school-teachers were women who had never become mothers because their prospective or actual husbands had died during the First World War. That generation was now reaching retirement and being replaced by women who had different expectations of life and, like Tutaev, had the benefit of relevant professional skills when they became mothers. At the 1974 AGM the PPA radically revised its official aims and named the involvement of parents in early education as a key objective. Other developments helped reinforce what they were saying. Young mothers were, for example, learning from the TV programme *Playschool* ways in which they could support their children's learning.

A VOICE FROM THE TIME

One mother's experience of the playgroup movement in the 1960s

I was an older mother, sitting at the breakfast table and reading the *Guardian*. The famous Belle Tutaev letter, which started it all in August 1961, was the spur for me to mention the possibility of starting a playgroup in Garden Village, near Wrexham, while at a birthday party in a friend's house nearby. It happened that one of us was a trained Nursery Teacher, so she gave us some professional advice. We called a meeting of all the mums living on one drive. So many came that we had to send out for a supply of picnic chairs . . .

The Playgroup opened in September, with equipment made, donated or borrowed, and the budget set on the basis of the number of children attending. From the beginning we held regular parents' meetings, took part in village events and supported other areas to do their own thing to provide pre-school education for their children . . .

Soon Wrexham had a branch of PPA and it helped form the County (Denbighshire) Branch, with a fair input to bringing Wales PPA into being.

So how was this achieved by groups of mothers in a continually evolving structure to meet the needs of under-fives?

First, it was the age-old commitment of parents to do their very best for their children and to be willing to learn what the best was . . .

Second, it was the realisation that we could only make progress if we worked together . . .

Third, we always, but always, sought professional advice.

Fourth, we were willing to travel beyond our area . . . to learn the range of skills needed to sustain the efforts which earned PPA a place in the network of services for children.

Fifth, we were supported by our families . . .

And what happened? Well, apart from building a network of pre-school groups throughout Wales, it gave a whole generation of mothers the confidence to support the community in all sorts of ways. There are many who would quote their experience in PPA as the basis of their achievements in many fields.

Source: This is an abbreviated version of a contribution by Marjorie Dykins to the book *Memories of the Playgroup Movement in Wales 1961–1987*, published by Wales PPA in 2008.

Developments in government policy in the 1960s

The PPA was a success story. Developments in the statutory sector were less impressive.

In 1963 the Children and Young Persons Act made provision – among other things – for Family Advice Centres to be set up by local children's departments. In some ways these projects were similar to the later Sure Start children's centres. The social work theorist Leissner believed they provided a way of re-inventing his profession, with their emphasis on advice, guidance and assistance rather than the 'phoney psychoanalysis' he thought had too much influence on social work practice. Whatever potential the centres may have had for transforming social work, they did not survive the re-organization of local authority social work services in 1971 and made little impression on the new social services departments (Leissner et al., 1971).

At about the time that the bill that became the 1963 Act was being debated, a committee was set up under Lady Plowden to consider the curriculum in nursery and primary schools. (A similar committee was established under the chairmanship of Professor Gittins for Wales.) The Plowden Report was not finished until 1966 and not published until the following year (DES, 1967). Its authors accepted Piaget's understanding of children's cognitive development and the implications of his work for the education of young children. Chapter 2 – Children, their growth and development – is quite explicit about this. Even relatively sympathetic critics have seen the report as being over-zealous in its reliance on Piaget's approach. The authors of the report supported expansion in nursery education, but wanted this to be offered on a part-time basis in nursery classes, partly because of assumptions about what was financially possible, partly because they did not wish to encourage the paid employment of mothers of young children. Even the expansion they were prepared to envisage was for the most part ditched because of the economic difficulties of the 1970s. The impact of Plowden on the primary school curriculum has been long-lasting and controversial. In terms of early childhood services it was yet another false dawn.

The third initiative taken in relation to early childhood services was a revision of the 1948 Nurseries and Childminders Act. The absence of any system of day care designed for working parents led to growth in both legal and illegal childminding. A Ministry of Health Inquiry in 1965 raised questions about the quality of childminding (Owen, 2006: 36). In particular, there were fears the large numbers of children taken by some childminders into homes that often relied – as many working-class homes did at the time – on free-standing paraffin and oil heaters created serious risks of accidental harm. A comprehensive piece of legislation on public health was planned for 1968 and, after some initial reluctance, it was agreed that the opportunity should be used to strengthen the regulation of childminders and private nursery care.

The principal change was an extension in the definition of 'childminder' so that more people had to seek registration. Joan Lester MP said in the Commons during the passage of the Bill, that it was unlikely that tougher regulation would by itself do much to improve the quality or availability of services (Owen, 2006: 39–40). The ways in which the relevant clauses of the Health Services and Public Health Act (1968) were implemented were often inadequate to ensure even effective regulation. Manchester City Council, to quote just one example, contented itself with placing a formal notice in the adverts section of the local evening newspaper. It is unlikely that many of the childminders who were working illegally read the notice carefully, if they saw it at all. Cllr Slight, a member of Hampshire City Council, declared that the Act was 'only a starter' (*Portsmouth Evening News*, 11/6/69). More than twenty years later Elfer and Beasley (1991) spelled out the numerous ways in which the legislation had not led to a satisfactory system of regulation.

The situation of early childhood services by the end of the 1960s

By 1969 the return to 'normality' that had been the height of ambition for many in 1945 had largely been achieved, but its very success was breeding a challenge that remained largely subterranean to that model of social existence.

HISTORY IN A NUTSHELL

The economic difficulties of the 1970s

The UK, like other wealthy nations, has been characterized, for some time by alternating periods of prosperity and economic downturn (or 'boom and bust' as it has sometimes been expressed). Economists differ as to whether this pattern just happens and might have been avoided altogether by wiser fiscal management or whether it is structurally inevitable and politicians should be content with getting through the process with as little distress as possible. If the pattern does have something inevitable about it, the UK was due for hard times in the 1970s, but people were so used to the constant rise in the standard of living since the late 1940s that even Marxists hesitated to predict another crisis. As things worked out, the 1970s experienced escalating economic and social difficulties. The social problems were aggravated as the economic ones grew worse. Revolutions happen, not because things are going badly, but because they no longer go as well as people have been led to expect. The 1970s saw many challenges to accepted opinion.

Women's liberation

In January 1969 the left-wing paper *Black Dwarf* declared that the year just starting would be 'the Year of the Militant Woman'. This editorial was not the main reason for what followed, but it can be taken as marking the beginning of the process. Several local radical women's groups were already in existence (taking their lead from middle-class feminist groups in the USA). The Women's Liberation Movement was launched as a more organized body with a number of basic demands at a conference in 1970.

One of the demands was for free, 24-hour nurseries for working mothers. This was a gift to the movement's enemies. It was often interpreted as a demand for nurseries where women could dump their children for days at a time. This went down badly with managers in the children's departments who were finally seeing off the residential nursery, which they regarded, with some reason, as a mistake. In fact, the demand had been for nurseries that would operate continually, so as to be available to parents who did not work the standard 9–5 day. The way it was presented played into the hands of those who believed that working mothers sacrificed the interests of their own children to their own wishes. Some of those who campaigned for nursery care gave insufficient attention to the type of care children should receive. On the other hand, there were notable exceptions, such as Valerie Charlton (1977) who helped to establish a community nursery in North London. The PPA was stronger for paying heed to the needs of children as well as those of the 'housebound housewife'. In spite of early propaganda errors, the demand for better childcare grew apace. In 1974 two trade unions, NALGO and NUPE (now both part of UNISON), launched the National Nursery Action Group. Towards the end of the decade feminist groups in London, having worked together for joint action in the capital, took steps to create a National Child Care Campaign.

Early childhood services and the 'cycle of deprivation'

Meanwhile, the 'rediscovery' of poverty by the academic world persuaded some politicians to modify the view that young children should stay at home with their mothers. Keith Joseph, one of the intellectual leaders of the Conservative Party, became convinced that the children of the poor remained poor in spite of the welfare state because the circumstances in which they were raised robbed them of the skills and dispositions they needed to advance themselves. There was thus a 'cycle of deprivation'. He made this argument forcefully in a series of speeches in the early 1970s and in his pamphlet *Caring for People* (1972). He was criticized by left-wing academics, such as Townsend, Jordan and Holman on the grounds that he confused different forms of disadvantage and exaggerated their interconnections (Welshman, 2006: 116–17). The cogency or otherwise of Joseph's analysis may have been less important to early childhood services than the fact that it led him to advocate expansion of provision in that field. He was a fan of the PPA. However, his support came at a price. It reinforced the notion that early childhood services should be offered primarily to families from deprived, poorly educated and maladjusted families, that they should be a compensatory rather than a universal kind of service. Pre-school Playgroups Association activists were constantly being told by social workers in the 1970s that they were too middle class and that their movement was really only needed in the poorest areas (Crowe, 1983: 7).

Early childhood services and cuts in public services

Apart from the question of whether it was a good idea in its own right, the restricted role devised for early childhood services made them once again vulnerable at a time of escalating economic crisis. It had been said often in the past that such services might be useful, but that we could not afford them in the current situation – a line of argument that concealed a value judgement under the cloak of apparent financial realism. At the beginning of the 1970s there were plans to expand both nursery education and nursery care. Then in 1974 Crosland, a minister in the recently elected Labour government, announced that the expansion of local authority services must end. He suggested that nursery education should be exempt from this general policy, but in the light of their overall financial problems many local authorities – particularly in rural areas, although also in London – decided to shelve or cancel plans they had for building new nursery schools and some existing ones were closed. The year in which the highest number ever of places in nursery schools was recorded came four years later in 1978. Since then the number has steadily declined.

Attempts were made to find ways of providing day care at low cost, the subject of a joint circular by the Department for Health and Social Security and the Department of Education and Science in 1976 and of a government-backed conference held at Sunningdale that year. Neither these nor any of the other efforts in the 1970s to find cheap ways of providing nursery care ever came to anything.

Nursery nursing and the new social services departments

The growing demand for early childhood services, along with the government's reluctance to provide them, had consequences for holders of NNEB qualifications. The number of places for nannies had declined since the late 1940s, partly because those who wanted that kind of domestic help discovered it was easier and cheaper to take on young foreign women as 'au pairs'. Nursery nurses had roles in schools and in some children's hospitals, but suffered from low status in those organizations. In some ways the best opportunities for the holders of NNEB qualifications seemed to lie with the social services departments that had come into existence in 1971 on the basis of an Act of Parliament passed the previous year.

In 1968 a committee of inquiry into personal social services had recommended that all local authority personal social services should be brought together (Seebohm, 1968). The committee had also suggested that 'Services for children under five should be considerably extended in both scope and flexibility' (para. 207). They accepted the established view that day care was a service primarily for parents in difficulty (paras 198–9), but they recognized the effect of pressures to get some women, especially in under-staffed statutory sectors such as teaching and nursing, back to work (para. 195). They also acknowledged that many parents wanted services for their children because this might open up wider experiences for them (para. 201). The Committee believed it was right and proper that day care services should be moved from the medical to the social services sphere (paras 202–3) and, as a consequence of that, argued that the social services departments should have responsibility for the regulation of the non-statutory sector. Both these recommendations were also written into the legislation.

Together with developments in training that were taking place, the creation of the social services departments might have bolstered both day care provision and the nursery nursing profession. One reason why this did not happen is that the new departments were tightly controlled by social workers, who now had an opportunity to establish their own profession on a more solid basis. Other occupational groups in the departments lost out. Moreover, the new departments were at the start dominated by managers from the former children's departments where the view that day care was a remedial measure for failing families was deeply entrenched. It was more or less impossible for staff in children's day care to rise very far in the management structure of the departments. In addition, the tight hierarchical organizational models that had developed in nurseries while they were under medical control survived and were even reinforced to protect the control of case management by field social workers. It was common in the early 1970s for basic grade nursery nurses to be forbidden to have any conversation with parents beyond the minimum that politeness would require. The opportunity for close collaboration between nursery nurses, who were engaged in the day-to-day care of children, and field social workers, who were supporting the children's parents, was not just lost, but deliberately discarded.

The crisis of confidence in nursery nursing

The low status of nursery nurses and the attendant problems came to a head in 1978 when the National Union of Public Employees (NUPE) attacked the NNEB's record on training and sought the support of the rest of the trade union movement in a campaign for change. Reg Race, who was then the head of NUPE, had the foresight to appreciate that nursery care was an issue of growing importance. NUPE was not the only critic of the NNEB. Others attacked it for failing to prepare students adequately for day care in a multiracial society. These assaults provoked a major crisis (Halloran, 1982: 76–7).

The NNEB responded by setting up its own independent review of its activity (Brierley Report, 1981) and instituting reforms at the board. The description of these events in Bessie Wright's more or less official history of the NNEB is accurate, but low key (Wright, 1999: 178–84). It reflects the tact and due consideration of different viewpoints that enabled her to be a successful chair of the board rather than the acrimony that was around. An unpublished thesis by Halloran (1982) offers a rather more animated account. At the time of the crisis she was running an NNEB course in Yorkshire and had been angered by NUPE's intervention. She attempts to rebuff the criticisms (not always convincingly, especially in relation to anti-racist work). However, an extensive survey of nursery nurses she conducted in her own region for her thesis persuaded her that there were aspects of the work for which nursery nurses were inadequately trained. These included report writing and communication with parents. Her survey also showed that, while the situation of nursery nurses in social services departments often felt unsatisfactory, staff in those departments were less anxious about their status than classroom assistants in schools (p. 103). The reason for this was probably that nursery nurses working in schools were under the direct supervision of teachers and, consequently, more conscious of status differences. Their colleagues in the social services departments did have a career structure of their own, even if it was limited. She makes the very astute suggestion (which proved prophetic in the 1980s) that shared membership of the trade union NALGO (National Association of Local Government Officers) might bring nursery nurses and field social workers closer together (p. 94). In the meanwhile professional development in nursery nursing remained patchy. Garland and White (1980) found wide variation in quality and practice in the nine (statutory and voluntary) nurseries in London that they studied.

The growth of the private sector

While the number of local authority day nurseries was kept low and those that were operating were designated as a service for families failing to cope, young mothers going out to work created a market for provision in the private sector. In 1968 Seebohm had spoken of the fact that the number of registered places in the private sector had grown five-fold in the period 1956–66 (para. 194). The pre-school playgroup movement must provide some of the explanation for this increase although sessional pre-schools did not offer an adequate day care service for mothers in paid employment. The real growth in the number of private nurseries came later – towards the end of the twentieth century. The early signs were obvious by the end of the 1970s.

The higher profile of childminding

For the time being the expansion of non-statutory nursery care was far outstripped by the number of childminders, both registered and unregistered.

In 1973, Brian and Sonia Jackson launched a research project on childminding in several areas of Britain. They produced valuable evidence of the extensive scale and dangerously poor quality of much illegal childminding and claimed that even registered childminders often lacked the skills, training and resources to meet their responsibilities adequately (Jackson and Jackson, 1979). What they wanted was more investment in childminding, but the evidence they unearthed helped to bring childminding into disrepute among many of the public and gave comfort to those, such as Bryant et al. (1980) who were arguing that care of children outside their families should occur as infrequently as possible.

The Jacksons set up the National Educational Research and Development Trust, a body that continued research in this area and held a series of national conferences on childminding, starting with one in Bradford in 1975 (Knight, 1975). Other developments followed.

The BBC produced a series of programmes on childminding under the title *Other People's Children* in 1976. Discussion groups were created to study the programmes. Some of them continued long after the initial study task was completed and other new groups of childminders joined them (Urben, 1977; Shinman, 1979).

The Community Relations Commission (1976) produced a report about childminding in black and minority ethnic communities.

NUPE attempted to recruit childminders as members and started a campaign to press for childminding to become a public service run by social services departments, as the home help service was at that time.

NUPE's approach attracted little support, but there was interest in some form of association. In 1977 the National Childminding Association (NCMA) was launched, not primarily as a body representing the interests of childminders, but in order to promote the childminding service and seek improvements in standards.

In several local authorities those responsible for the regulation of childminding began to extend their role (often with little backing from senior management) in order to offer childminders greater support. Some local authorities created specialist adviser posts to work alongside childcare inspectors.

Other developments

Two other developments characterized the 1970s.

One was new research. The Victorians had been assiduous gatherers of information and the creation of a universal elementary education system facilitated the collection of statistics about children. It was not until the 1970s (following the development of university undergraduate courses in the social sciences) that research based on the testing of hypotheses started to become a key element in the elaboration of policy. In 1971 the Department for Education and Science in England and Wales and the Scottish Education Department sponsored research on nursery education that led to a Pre-School Research Group headed in Oxford by the American Jerome Bruner (1980). Apart from the influential Oxford studies, there were also reports on early childhood services published by the Office of Population, Censuses and Surveys (Bone, 1977) and the Central Policy Review Staff (1978).

The second development was a growing appreciation of the difficulties caused by the diversity of agencies involved in early childhood services. Responsibility was split between education and social services departments and the NHS. Departments within local authorities and in Whitehall tended to look after their own affairs, to cooperate with each other in very restricted ways and neglect the coordinated planning of new provision. This was reflected in early research on services. Projects often took as their subject specific types of setting (day nurseries, childminding, etc.). There were few attempts to compare different types to see whether potentially complementary roles could be defined.

Although the most important changes on the ground did not begin until after the 1970s, a number of generalized policy statements were issued, urging local authorities to take a more comprehensive approach. In 1973 DES Circular 2/73 called on them to be more conscious of the contribution of the voluntary sector when planning expansion. In 1976 both the DHSS and DES issued a circular on *Co-ordination of Local Authority Services for Children Under Five* (DHSS/DES 1976b), following this up in 1978 with another circular on coordination, this time asking them to take community health services and the independent sector into account. In the meanwhile the DES floated the idea of combined nursery schools and day centres. Early childhood services were still seen as peripheral and there was still a particular focus on the needs of families that were coping badly, but the ground was being laid for a new approach to provision.

The end of consensus

The steps taken towards improvement in early childhood services that were made by central and local government were only tentative, but offered some grounds for optimism. This did not last. Hope was undermined by the escalating economic crisis of the decade and other indications that post-war 'normality' was breaking down – militant trade unionism, armed conflict in Northern Ireland, the Women's Liberation Movement, the growing assertiveness of black organizations, and changes in attitudes to the family, sexuality and drugs. Some said Britain had become 'ungovernable', might even fall victim to a military *coup d'état*. Any possibility of reformed and expanded early childhood services seemed likely to be swamped by some general breakdown in society and the state.

Exercise

With the close of this chapter, the story of early childhood services has reached the point where many of those involved in such services (as clients, practitioners or policy-makers) are still around. Ask someone who was involved in an early years setting before 1980 what the situation was like then and what that person believes makes it different from or similar to the present day.

Further reading

Clarke's (2004) *Hope and Glory*, which was recommended in the previous chapter, is also recommended for the period covered by this chapter.

Charmley's history of the Conservative Party (2008) offers convincing explanations for both the consensus on the welfare state in the 1950s and 1960s and the collapse of that consensus at the end of the 1970s.

Wilson's book *Women and the Welfare State* (1977) is still a relevant description of developments in early childhood and other services for most of the twentieth century. It is also a useful 'primary source', coming as it does out of the feminist movement of the 1970s.

Wright's (1999) history of the NNEB is an important source on one aspect of the history of nursery nursing.

Whitbread's (1972) history of nursery and infant education, which has already been recommended for earlier periods, offers a useful guide for most of the period covered by this chapter.

4   The development of early childhood services after the breakdown of consensus (1979–1997)

In the event the United Kingdom did not get a military dictator in 1979 – it got Margaret Thatcher instead. That was not quite the same thing, in spite of the fact that she enjoyed being filmed riding in a tank and built her commanding position in politics through success in the Falklands War. In several respects the changes that Thatcher secured were more significant and longer lasting than a military dictator might have attempted (Jenkins, 2007).

This chapter describes:

- the principal features of social policy during the Conservative governments of Margaret Thatcher and John Major;
- the growing demand for childcare and new confidence in its potential;
- indecision about nursery education within government;
- the new regulatory system for day care and childminding under the 1989 Children Act;
- the development of ideas about inter-professional collaboration in early childhood services.

Thatcherism and social policy

It was not appreciated at first that the Conservative victory in the general election of 1979 meant a decisive turn from post-war consensus on social policy. After all, when the Conservatives had been elected in 1971, they had intended to bring about a more market-driven economic regime and that attempt had failed. Moreover, the continuing conflicts in Northern Ireland and Southern Rhodesia (now Zimbabwe) seemed likely to dominate events and to impede any major reshaping of the welfare state. The turn to the right might prove to be a temporary aberration, to be followed by a return to the post-war consensus or even a further shift to the left.

Such opinions underestimated Thatcher's deep personal commitment to reversing the values of the consensus and the way that resonated with much of what later came to be called 'Middle England'. She rejected the very idea of public service. In her view, those who claimed dedication to it were being dishonest, trying to conceal the ways in which they were making personal gains at the tax payers' expense or the fact that they were losers unable to make it in business. Someone holding such opinions could not be expected to admire those who dedicated themselves to nursery education and care – an area of service provision that had never been a way of making serious money. She was also happy to ditch the post-war commitment to full employment. Her belief was that a sound economy would in the long run create employment opportunities for those who really wanted them and special measures to protect employment were an obstacle to achieving this. Jobs were most at risk in the older, male-dominated, manufacturing industries. Thus it was unclear what the impact of her policy would be on women's employment, but some were afraid it would diminish opportunities for them and one of the consequences of this might have been a levelling out of the demand for childcare.

Social policy was considerably recast with cuts in welfare benefits, the sale of council houses to their tenants, the creation of a National Curriculum, the replacement of the former schools inspection service in England and Wales by Ofsted and the gradual return to specialization by client grouping in the social services departments. Existing policy on early childhood settings (discouraging mothers from using full day care to seek paid work and concentrating the attention of services on dysfunctional families) could be expected to be part of the package. After all, the Conservatives were committed to 'family values'. There were numerous statements by ministers regretting the breakdown in the old division of labour within the nuclear family. Some policies followed that direction, such as the attempt to prevent what the Conservatives saw as the 'promotion' of homosexuality or the rise in the number of single parent families. The way to secure full-scale return to the post-war family was elusive, but they did attempt it.

The difficulty they faced was that the aspiration of families to secure a better standard of living – an aspiration the Conservatives endorsed – led many women with small children to seek paid work. Indeed, economic difficulties made this essential if they were to maintain the standard of living they had already achieved. The demand for childcare continued to grow. At the same time the success of the PPA and the growing self-confidence of nursery teachers bolstered a trend to re-evaluate early education. It was now often seen as the necessary foundation stone for children's later achievement. The period 1979–1997 witnessed new demands for early childhood services and a few measures by the government and by pioneering local authorities that laid the basis for a major alteration of policy on early childhood after 1997.

The demand for childcare and developments in provision

Private day nurseries were a more expensive form of childcare than child-minding, but the bad publicity childminding had attracted in the 1970s encouraged parents to turn to them. By the end of the 1980s growth in the sector was sufficiently evident to produce concern that it would fatally undermine the case for universal childcare provided by the state (Bond, 1989).

There were suggestions that larger companies could be persuaded to provide childcare services directly to their employees. Some did so, including British Rail and Midland Bank (now part of HSBC). Such arrangements were explicitly for working parents and thus avoided the stigma that attached to social services nurseries. However, most employers were unwilling to meet the expense (Parrock, 1989). In addition, changes in the system of income tax in 1983 robbed many parents of the tax advantages of using workplace nurseries. (This resulted from moves by the Inland Revenue to tighten up loopholes in the system rather than any desire to discourage mothers from paid work, but it added to the difficulties working mothers faced.) A Workplace Nurseries Campaign was launched the following year, but secured few victories (Williamson, 1989).

In spite of the obstacles, the impressive expansion in the number of private nurseries continued. There were also new initiatives in the voluntary sector. Many established charities had already turned from maternity and child welfare services to day care. In 1960 the City of Westminster Health Society (WHS), having closed down the year before the one nursery it had run since the 1920s, had opened the first of its 'toddler clubs'. (They may have chosen that term to avoid the stigma that now attached to the word 'nursery'.) With the health service reorganization of 1974 the agency lost many of its health care functions and changed its name a couple of years later to 'Westminster Children's Society' (Harrison and Barnett, 1983). As its current name (the London Early Years Foundation) suggests, it is now essentially in the business of providing pre-school education and care. Often it was not established charities, such as the WHS, that undertook day care for children, but new community-based agencies that saw themselves as part of a movement demanding better childcare. Examples include the Sheffield Children's Centre and Joseph's Nursery in York.

1991 was the peak year for the number of registered childminders. It is important not to read too much into this. By 1993 the process of re-registration of existing minders required by the 1989 Children Act had revealed that many who had been on local authority registers for ages were no longer minding, in some cases had actually died. However, after 1991 the long, slow process started by which both legal and illegal minding ceased to be the principal form of childcare outside the family.

Different types of care were opening. During the 1970s a large number of open access playschemes had been initiated, at first run mostly by local authorities or established voluntary agencies, such as Save The Children, later by more community-based bodies (similar, therefore, to the PPA). Holiday playschemes provided care during the day, but they were usually designed to offer new opportunities for children rather than a service for working mothers. The case was made for day care out of school hours for children over 5. Requests from parents led to after-school clubs being started in schools or other buildings, such as church halls. Playschemes had often received small grants from their local authority recreation departments. Once after-school clubs became part of the childcare scene, national funding became available. What had usually started as informal community-based projects became more professional.

Things were also changing in the PPA. Its success and the growing market for day nurseries raised the question of whether the Association or its affiliates should branch out into full day care (Sloane, 1989). Fears that the organization was abandoning its original vision led some to form the Playgroup Network, in 1991. This achieved a strong following on Tyneside and in several other areas, but it never replaced the organization from which it had parted in terms of influence on national policy.

New national organizations

Non-statutory provision prompted the creation of several new agencies to support the sector.

- In 1980 a National Child Care Campaign was launched. The solid base it had among feminist groups in London proved an obstacle in some ways to securing a wider following outside the capital, so that over the decade it faded away at least as a separate organization. The wish to attract money to some of the less obviously political activities in which the campaign was involved led to the creation in 1986 of a charity, the Day Care Trust, which became an important feature of the national childcare scene.
- In 1982 the National Out of School Alliance (later to be called the Kids Clubs Network, later still 4Children) was launched as an independent body.
- In 1987 a children's information service was opened in Sheffield, specifically as a pilot for a possible nationwide provision of similar services.

- In 1989 the National Children's Bureau set up the Early Childhood Forum, a network that became an important mechanism for interprofessional exchange and the campaign for better-coordinated early childhood services.
- In 1990 a Childcare Association, representing private nursery proprietors, began work. However, this was not as strong a body as some of the others mentioned and in 2000 the National Day Nurseries Association effectively replaced it.
- In the meantime the National Childminding Association (NCMA), launched in 1977, was growing steadily in strength and influence and establishing productive relationships with under-5s advisers in the social services departments.

The response of the political parties

These developments outside the statutory sector highlighted the growing demand for early childhood services and the self-confidence of those who provided them. The Labour Party believed the state at national and local level should adopt a new, more active role. In 1985 it issued a policy statement on the subject. The fact that another twelve years passed before the Labour Party won a general election meant that some of the ambitious plans in that document never came to fruition. Nevertheless, it continued to influence party policy on the subject in the years before 1997.

The Conservatives gradually reconciled themselves to the existence of career women whose children might need care from people other than their mothers. Thatcher was, after all, a career woman herself, although the solution she found in her own case (marrying a businessman wealthy enough to employ nannies without a second thought) was not open to many. The Party still failed to see much of a role for the state in the provision of day nurseries beyond cheering on the voluntary and private sectors. Their spokesman Roger Freeman made this crystal clear at a conference in 1985 organized jointly by the Association of Metropolitan Authorities, the Association of County Councils and the National Campaign for Voluntary Child Care Organisations.

Nursery education

The government felt a little differently about pre-school education. Margaret Thatcher held Sir Keith Joseph in high regard and made him her first Secretary of State for Education. She took note of his idea that pre-school education had a potentially important part to play in opening up opportunities for advancement to children from poorer families, although never strongly enough to develop a detailed interest in the topic, in spite of the fact that she had been at one time Secretary of State for Education.

Those Conservatives who were interested in the evidence took note of reports that raised some problematic issues, but also provided new evidence on the value of pre-school education. Osborn and Milbank (1989) undertook research that compared outcomes (particularly in terms of behaviour) of children attending different kinds of settings and produced valuable evidence on this. They found little evidence that pre-school education affected later behaviour for better or worse. They did uncover some evidence that children aged 10 who had attended local authority day nurseries were more likely to have emotional or behavioural difficulties, but ascribed this to the criteria for entry to local authority day nurseries rather than the impact of the settings themselves. Like other research, theirs provided some material for those parts of the media that were hostile to early years day care. Overall, however, it helped to undermine the notion that nursery care was a cause of later problems. There were also important reports commissioned by the government itself. Clark in her 1987 report showed herself reluctant to challenge the idea that the primary function of early childhood services was to compensate for deficiencies in families. However, her survey was wide-ranging and had important findings on the ways in which settings could assist black and minority ethnic children, on approaches to work with children with special needs and on the potential benefits of improved coordination of services. In 1990 the Rumbold Committee of Inquiry similarly called for closer coordination and spoke of the role central government could have in developing better routes to qualification. Above all, it achieved a crucial victory in seeing off the idea of introducing the new National Curriculum in nursery classes and schools.

In spite of all this, the governments of Thatcher and Major were disinclined to invest in early childhood services. The number of nursery schools continued to diminish. Where the government took initiatives that had a positive impact, they were often not designed with the early years especially in mind. For example, the Education Act of 1981 established the principle of inclusion in the school system for children with special educational needs. This influenced practice in early years settings, but the policy was devised for schools. Even the voucher scheme for nursery education places developed just before the end of Conservative rule was probably intended as a pilot for the full-blown use of vouchers throughout the education system rather than to support nursery education. (Sir Keith Joseph had disapproved of the idea of education vouchers in the 1970s. He believed they would be used most effectively by the best-educated parents and would, as a result, provide another welfare state benefit to the more affluent rather than a means of helping the disadvantaged. He was converted to the idea of vouchers in the 1980s, but nothing was done about this until some time later.) The one truly important step taken by the Conservative government was a radical reform of regulation.

Regulation and the Children Act, 1989

The research undertaken by the Jacksons and others cast doubt on the effectiveness of the legislation passed in 1948 and revised in 1968. Regulation seemed incapable of preventing widespread bad practice and had done little to promote improvement in standards. Nothing might have happened, but for the fact that the government felt pressed to introduce changes in the law on children in the light of notorious examples of failures in the child protection system. Something had been attempted after the death of Maria Colwell and the subsequent outrage at what had happened to her, but the Children Act (1975) was too timid a measure – a missed opportunity. In 1988, the Conservatives proposed more radical measures in a parliamentary bill that also replaced the old concept of parental rights with a new one of parental responsibility and articulated more clearly and coherently existing law on the rights of families from religious and ethnic minorities when the state had occasion to intervene in their affairs. Initially, there was no intention to include a further revision of the 1948 Act. However, NCMA joined with 16 other organizations to create a pressure group called Law Reform for Children's Day Care to demand such a change. The bill acquired a new Part X dealing with the regulation of day care and childminding. As well as strengthening the law in several respects, the Act extended the number of services required to seek registration by making the relevant age range 0–8 years rather than 0–5.

Some voluntary organizations had pressed for an age range of 0–16 years. Such a step might have improved services for older children. It was, however, probably helpful to early childhood services that the legislation passed focused attention much more clearly on them. The new regulatory regime gave childcare inspectors a higher profile than they had had before. The fact that changes to regulation were made part of a major piece of legislation on children drew the attention of senior management in social services departments to the issue. This effect was reinforced by the production of more detailed guidelines on implementation than had been offered in 1948 or 1968 (Department of Health, 1991) and by the training pack for inspectors commissioned by the government from the National Children's Bureau (Early Childhood Unit, 1991). Moreover, in spite of the reservations that many Conservative MPs had about the care of young children outside the family home, the Act came at a time when public opinion was swinging in favour of early childhood services and wanted guarantees that they were properly run.

This did not mean that everything ran smoothly (Baldock, 2001: 8–14). Local authorities had difficulty in getting new regulatory systems off the ground and some failed to meet the deadlines set for them. Playcare services were new territory for most existing childcare inspectors who were sometimes baffled by open access playschemes and adventure playgrounds and the ways in which they differed from the nurseries and playgroups to which they were more accustomed. A number of court cases left local authority childcare inspectors feeling vulnerable, undermined and uncertain about the extent of their authority. A circular issued at the beginning of 1993 was critical of what the government considered to be over-stringent regulation and there were signs that the Conservatives were having second thoughts about inspection by local authority staff as a way of guaranteeing quality to fee-paying consumers of services. They had seen regulation as a way of preventing worst practice and were less than happy that some local authority inspectors were using the new system to push for a general improvement in quality.

In spite of this the Conservatives never abandoned the idea that regulation of day care and childminding was required as a consumer protection device. Similarly, they were anxious that parents should receive value for money when they exchanged their nursery education vouchers. A document describing the 'desirable outcomes' of pre-school education published by the Department for Education and Employment and the School Curriculum and Assessment Authority in 1996 provided the criteria under which settings would be assessed for their suitability to receive the new vouchers. This was the first step towards creating an official curriculum for what would later be called the Foundation Stage.

The changing situation of nursery nursing

Staff members in local authority nurseries were routinely asked to deal with some of the consequences of serious family difficulties or even child abuse. In spite of this, policy-makers were reluctant to draw the conclusion that nursery nursing was or should be a highly skilled profession. Things were different in the case of nursery education. The tradition stretching back to the nineteenth century that the education of very young children required professional expertise and commitment was too well established by the beginning of the twentieth century to be dislodged easily.

New ideas about early childhood services undermined the assumption that care and education were separate activities. Some of this came from what was happening in settings themselves. Managers of the day nursery service in individual settings and in the central offices of social services departments advocated a new role for the nursery nurse. The more it became possible to have confidence that most children would be healthy, the more irrelevant some of the rigid regimes based on older models of hospital care were seen to be. Greater informality in social relationships in the wider society encouraged more interaction between nursery nurses and the parents or social workers of the children for whom they were caring. The concept of the key worker emerged from the practice of the best settings and was developed with the assistance of research work by the Thomas Coram Foundation and other bodies. The attention that had been paid to childcare by NUPE in the 1970s and the role assumed by many field social workers as elected NALGO officials created a new basis for communication and mutual respect between nursery nurses and the dominant profession in the social services departments. Some were unhappy with this aspect of the way things were going. Nursery nurses who found militant trade union activity alienating formed the Professional Association of Nursery Nurses. There was, nevertheless, a positive impact in many departments. Ideas from the world of nursery education started to influence courses leading to qualification in day nursery work. This escalated in 1994 when the NNEB merged with the Council for Early Years Awards to form the Council for Awards in Children's Care and Education (CACHE).

If the statutory sector was changing slowly, the private and voluntary sector was even more open to new ideas. Most private nurseries catered for better-educated and ambitious parents and were well aware that they needed to provide for children's learning if they were to please their clients. The Conservatives' plans for a nursery voucher scheme underlined that fact.

Childminding was more problematic in this respect. On the one hand, the NCMA was working hard to improve the standards and profile of childminding. On the other hand, the poor image with which childminding had been saddled in the 1970s inhibited the kind of self-esteem that is essential to professionalism. A further difficulty was that many local authority childcare inspectors had seen the recruitment of childminders as a way of securing resources for social work colleagues and modelled their approach to the task of regulation on that of support to foster parents. This led to some imaginative activity, but it did so at the cost of perpetuating the dependence of childminders on their inspectors in a way that created a barrier to professional independence. That situation persisted throughout the period of Conservative rule and took some time to change after 1997. In spite of this, there was a growing sense of what their role might entail among childminders – one that took the Labour government by surprise in 2001 when it tried to exempt them from some of the standards required of day care staff.

The demand to end fragmentation

The growing professionalism of nursery nurses and childminders and the renewed self-confidence of nursery teachers rendered the rigid separation of care and education problematic. Official documents from the 1970s and 1980s had often spoken of collaboration between early childhood services. This became a dominant theme in academic writing on such services from the late 1980s to the early 1990s (Pugh, 1988; David, 1994).

Teachers had more self-confidence than nursery staff, something that became very clear to Anning and Edwards (1999: 81) in their work with both staff groups. It came to be assumed that education would be the lead profession in any coordinated early years services (Goldschmied and Jackson, 1994: 36). Of course, giving the lead role to an established profession was always going to be far easier and less disruptive, expensive or controversial than trying to create a brand new profession of early years practitioners, of the kind envisaged by Peter Moss and some other commentators.

Given the uncertain development of early childhood services in the UK since the war, many people looked abroad for alternative models and for evidence that their ideas would work in practice. Helen Penn, who had been a leading figure in the National Child Care Campaign, compared practice here unfavourably with what she had seen in Spain and Italy (Penn, 1997). Others spoke of developments in Scandinavia and New Zealand. It was sometimes implied that the UK was out of step with everyone else, at least in the developed world. This was far from the case. In addition to several European countries, the United States had a similar separation of care and education. That is the reason why the USA provided less inspiration than might have been expected given the common language, the impact of Bruner's stay in Oxford and the interest here in the American Head Start approach.

One of the requirements of the Children Act (1989) was that local authorities in Britain should conduct annual reviews of arrangements for day care and childminding in their areas – something that focused attention on the lack of coherence in the planning and delivery of services. Many local authorities had already set up committees bringing together elected members and officers from various departments to co-ordinate work for the under-5s. In addition, there were a few examples of 'integrated' settings. The most famous of these was at Pen Green in Corby, which opened in 1983. Such projects entailed much more than organizational coordination. They became important centres of innovation (Makins, 1997). Work on partnership with parents was just one area where Pen Green led the field (Whalley, 2007).

A VOICE FROM THE TIME

An example of a developing consensus on the need for better coordination of services

The passage below is an extract from a report outlining proposals for a corporate childcare strategy in Sheffield written in 1992. What is said is typical of approaches being adopted in authorities run by the Labour Party in the early 1990s.

Publicly funded childcare services historically have been developed from two separate strands of concern and activity – the one relating to the health and safety of children, the other to children's education . . . Both types of service have, during their development, seen the needs of children as paramount, but this approach has sometimes ignored the impact made by the unmet needs of parents on the lives of their children. Both the division between services and the 'children only' emphasis have . . . caused facilities and services to be less than ideal in meeting the whole range of family support needs. It is now generally accepted that children's services have to include intrinsic recognition of and support to parental need, and that the division between welfare and educational issues is largely a false one.

In some local authorities things went further than the launching of projects in particular neighbourhoods, with new 'integrated' services being created within education departments. The first of these was in Strathclyde in 1986, with Helen Penn as its head. When the Labour Party lost the general election of 1992 and it became clear that it would have to wait for an opportunity to change the direction of national policy, several Labour-controlled Councils in England set up similar units so as to take things some way forward.

Conclusion

Early childhood services were not a priority for the Conservatives in the 1980s and 1990s. It was the continuing changes in the pattern of family life that really influenced services for young children. In that context those who worked in early childhood began to develop once again a measure of confidence in the importance of their work and the support for it in many sectors of society. Inventive approaches to organization and practice were adopted in several places. Some of this happened because of the initiatives of basic grade staff in the social services departments. Some of it involved new structural arrangements set up by councillors. Change was demanded by a whole set of new national bodies and by academics in what was essentially a new area of teaching and research. The way was open for a transformation of early childhood services. The opportunity for that came when the Labour Party won the general election of 1997.

Exercise

Select a setting that you know that was in existence in the early 1980s. Construct a systematic comparison between the way it was run then and the way it is run now. The setting's record system and the personal memories of those who have been associated with it for some time should help you to do this. What has changed for the better? What, if anything, has got worse? What remains unchanged? What do those involved in the earlier period see as the principal drivers of change? How does this pattern of change at a very local level compare with the national picture provided by this book?

Further reading

Tricia David's *Working Together for Young Children* (1994) was intended to influence opinion at the time. It now offers a useful picture of ideas in the early years professions at the beginning of the 1990s when the Conservatives still had a few years left in power.

5 The new emphasis on early childhood (1997–2001)

It is said that general elections are lost rather than won. Certainly, the brief period of euphoria that greeted the Labour Party's victory in May 1997 had less to do with enthusiasm for the winners than relief that an 18-year period of control by one particular party was at an end. Blair had re-branded his party as 'New Labour', although he stopped short of trying to secure a formal alteration of the name. The leaders of the party no longer talked about the working class as they had done in 1945, preferring to praise individual 'hard-working families'. The objective was now to support such families to achieve the things they wanted for themselves and to encourage or brow-beat those that were less hard working to join them.

This chapter describes:

- the uncertain nature of Blair's commitment to reform of early childhood services;
- the cautious approach to change that characterized his government's initial policy stance;
- the introduction of the National Childcare Strategy;
- the steps that were taken on nursery education;
- the search for improved coordination in the planning and delivery of early childhood services;
- the plans for a new system of regulation of day care and childminding;
- some developments outside government;
- the significance of devolution for early childhood services.

Initial difficulties over childcare policy

Advocates of a new deal for early childhood were among those happiest with the election result. The Labour Party had an unusually high number of women MPs. Most had been active in, or at least influenced by, the Women's Liberation Movement when they were younger and they were expected to press for better childcare.

Given the expectations, it is striking how little interest in childcare Blair himself expressed. Books that record his time in power sympathetically or from advantage points within Whitehall just do not mention the subject. Examples include Rentoul (2001), Seldon (2004), Campbell (2007) and Boulton (2008). The impression this leaves is reinforced by what Blair had to say when he outlined his vision for government just before the election (Blair, 1996). Early childhood services receive one brief mention (on p. 68) where he talks about childcare being one of several ways of supporting single parents back into paid work, so that they can become 'citizens of new Britain'. Thatcher's government had been inclined to prefer that mothers of young children stay at home, even if they were single parents, but Blair's perspective on childcare as a way of getting parents off benefits was not one that differentiated him from Conservatives. Norman Tebbitt, on the right of the Conservative Party, had also thought there was a good case for a policy of subsidizing childcare in order to get people off benefits and into work (Tebbitt, 1991: 133).

The prime minister's lack of interest need not have been decisive. After all, when the public health system was being comprehensively reformed in 1875, Disraeli, who was then prime minister, seems to have regarded the whole issue with distant amusement. There were members of Blair's first Cabinet who did regard early childhood services as valuable, including – crucially – Gordon Brown, the Chancellor of the Exchequer. David Blunkett, Blair's first Secretary of State for Education, describes him as having 'spotted very clearly' that childcare was going to be a major issue in the coming decade (Blunkett, 2006: 28).

Blair's lack of interest in the details of childcare policy caused him to become easily impatient with the fact that progress was slow. He seems to have believed that it was a simple administrative task to make childcare widely available and that it should be sorted out in next to no time. In fact, he toyed with the idea that things might go better if his party reversed the policy it had adopted in opposition and took responsibility for childcare away from the Department for Education and Employment (DFEE). He probably did not appreciate the implications, but this demonstrates how out of sympathy he was with the majority of early years professionals on this matter. By December 1999 Blunkett was worried that responsibility for childcare would be transferred to the Department of Health and that, if that were to happen, early childhood services would be 'aimed purely at the disadvantaged in the old-fashioned professional way' (Blunkett, 2006: 156–7). Blunkett may have been unaware that throughout the century it had often been early years professionals who had wanted services to be universal and politicians who had believed that they should be there primarily to help the disadvantaged. On the other hand, he may have had the social work profession specifically in mind. His first political post of any importance had been as chair of the social services committee in Sheffield.

Ultimately, the decision to move early childhood services from Education to Health was never taken. The transfer would have deprived the DfEE of the money set aside for childcare. As a result the UK would have missed a target Blair had set of matching the expenditure of other European Union countries on education (Blunkett, 2006: 151–2). The cost of boosting the general Education budget by the amount lost to Health would have been considerable and out of key with the government's vaunted financial 'prudence'. This made the transfer to Health impossible. If it *had* taken place, it would have been extraordinarily significant and probably led to a wholesale return to older concepts of public services for young children. The frightening thing is that the issue was settled, not on its own merits, but to make the accounts look good.

A VOICE FROM THE TIME

Extracts from the Executive Summary of the Green Paper *Meeting the Childcare Challenge*

These extracts illustrate how the strategy devised by Blunkett and others went beyond merely enabling parents to come off benefit and return to paid work:

Our children must get the best start in life. Families must be given genuine choices: to look after their children full-time or to combine work, education or training with parenting in a balanced way. Good quality childcare can help with this. Good quality care isn't merely about caring for children, but about introducing them to the joys of imaginative play, a love of books and a diverse and exciting range of sporting activities. Good quality care stimulates and motivates children. . . . Parents will always have the primary responsibility for the care and well-being of their children. It is up to parents to decide what sort of childcare they want for their children. This is not a matter for Government. But it is the Government's responsibility to ensure that parents have access to services to enable them to make genuine choices. This means good quality, affordable childcare for parents who wish to work outside the home and support for parents, relatives and other informal carers who look after children.

Caution in the development of early years policy

In 2001, on the eve of another general election, Moss complained that 'Blunkett and other Government figures have missed an opportunity to rethink early childhood services' (p. 10). His elucidation of the issues that had been inadequately addressed since 1997 is clear and compelling. However, in putting the blame for this on David Blunkett and Margaret Hodge, he underestimated the conflict within the government. To a large extent the failure to move forward decisively arose from the effectively concealed dispute between those who saw childcare simply as a way of encouraging people on benefits back to work and those who had wider objectives similar to those of Moss himself, if less fervently held.

It was not just the problem of managing differences of opinion within the Cabinet that led ministers to move slowly. Gordon Brown was determined to exercise financial restraint in the period immediately after the election because he wanted to reassure people that 'New' Labour would not return to the leftward leaning policies of the 1970s and 1980s which had proved unpopular with most of 'Middle England'. This made it difficult to devote too much additional money to childcare. The Cabinet were also wary of offending the tabloid press (most of which had only recently come round to tolerating the Labour Party) by measures that might challenge conventional views on the family. Whatever the reasons, progress was – as Moss says – exceedingly slow.

The National Childcare Strategy

The first major step taken was to outline a National Childcare Strategy. There was no question of what might have been seen as the traditionally 'socialist' solution of a universal system of state-provided day nurseries. Of course, there would have been nothing particularly 'socialist' about such a measure. France had something of the sort and both Left and Right approved of it in principle, while disagreeing about some of the details. There was a similar consensus in other European countries. However, fear of what the press would make of a new large-scale statutory service, together with considerations of financial caution, led Blunkett and his colleagues to plan a system under which the state supported childcare that was for the most part provided by the private and voluntary sectors.

The government's strategy for childcare was spelled out in the Green Paper *Meeting the Childcare Challenge* issued in 1998 (DFEE, 1998). This consultation document spoke of the way that childcare helped families to give their children the best start in life and said that grandparents and other members of the extended family could no longer be relied upon to undertake this work because of changing family circumstances. The Green Paper described three major problems:

- variability in the quality of the childcare on offer;
- the difficulties many families had in meeting the costs;
- the lack of places and the lack of easily accessible information on the places that did exist.

The strategy that was outlined was based on the principle of offering as much choice as possible to parents. This entailed a reversal of one of the principal features of the welfare state during the post-war consensus – that professionals and politicians had the responsibility of deciding what people needed and then gave it to them. The idea that the public were consumers who wanted to shop around for childcare and other public services in much the same way as they did for a better kind of chocolate biscuit came to characterize Labour Party policy. Little time was spent on checking how much of a priority this was to most people.

The key elements of the strategy were related to the problems that had been identified:

- raising the quality of care by better regulation, improvements in the training and education of practitioners and greater integration of day care with early education (with projects called early excellence centres funded by central government providing a model);
- making childcare more affordable, primarily by a new childcare tax credit for working families together with some special arrangements for parents who were in education and training;
- making new funding available to encourage the development of additional places.

The growth in the private sector, which had been underway for a while, escalated. The number of new applications for registration being handled by childcare inspectors increased noticeably. A new body representing independent nurseries – the National Day Nurseries Association – was launched.

Early education

By speaking of a National Childcare Strategy rather than a strategy for early childhood services, the government demonstrated that it intended to move slowly towards an integration of care, education and family support. In fact, it was the Home Office that assumed responsibility at first for family support, publishing a document on this in 1998. Nevertheless, *Meeting the Childcare*

Challenge suggested the direction of change by speaking of the importance of integrating care and education.

The government introduced reforms in the sphere of nursery education itself. The voucher scheme the Conservatives had devised was scrapped and replaced by one of nursery grants. The intention was to retain the principle of parental choice while avoiding the kind of competition the vouchers had been intended to encourage. Instead of being rivals, providers in the statutory and independent sectors were expected to cooperate with each other. In practice cooperation proved problematic. It was not long before independent providers were complaining that primary schools were setting themselves up in competition with them in order to secure their own sustainability. They claimed that schools that did this disregarded the interests of other providers of pre-school services and put unfair pressure on parents who wanted to be on good terms with the schools their children were likely to attend once they were 5.

In addition to introducing nursery grants, the government produced new curriculum guidance for what was now called the 'Foundation Stage' (QCA/DfEE, 2000). This was an improvement on the earlier initiatives. Serious difficulties remained. The government's measures to improve literacy and numeracy in primary schools often created (as similar demands made on primary school teachers had done throughout the twentieth century) downward pressure on pre-school settings to adopt inappropriately formal teaching methods. The fact that many schools chose to label their nursery classes 'FS1' and 'FS2' was indicative. Moreover, the guidance issued in 2000 only dealt with children in their third and fourth years. This had two implications. It suggested the government might be thinking of following the example of some other European countries (among them Belgium, France, Italy, Luxembourg and the Netherlands) and might divide early childhood provision into care before the age of 3 and education thereafter. It also represented yet another failure to challenge the 1870 decision that 5 was the age at which formal education should begin.

The search for coherence

There had been tentative moves towards improving the coordination of early childhood services since the 1970s, mainly within local authorities under Labour control. Now it was in power at national level the Labour Party was able to take this forward. The measures introduced were all related to the idea of securing greater coherence (or 'joined-up thinking' as it was sometimes described) in the planning of services.

A system of spending reviews was instituted to ensure that all expenditure was in line with government policy. For the most part reviews were conducted on a department-by-department basis. Early childhood was different. Several departments had some responsibility. A review group was established under Tessa Jowell, the Minister for Public Health, to coordinate work on reviewing expenditure on early childhood.

Some responsibilities were transferred to the DfEE, although at first the distinction between care and education was retained in funding and other programmes within that department.

Local authorities were required to establish formal partnerships to develop childcare, building on an earlier government initiative. The relevant local authority departments, community health services, providers of day care in the independent sector and parents were all to be included. The performance, even the membership, of the Early Years Development and Childcare Partnerships (EYDCPs) varied enormously. After 2001 the government was to decide that the EYDCPs could not be the mainstay of progress. The experiment with them was, however, an example of what the government meant by the 'third way', steering a path between extending statutory provision and leaving everything to the market.

The Local Government Act (2000) was informed by similar notions. It gave local authorities new responsibilities to promote the general well-being of people in their areas and to establish mechanisms for coordination between the local authorities themselves, other statutory agencies and the private and voluntary sectors on a whole range of issues. This was to be taken further forward after Blair's second election victory in 2001.

Finally, the government funded projects to develop early childhood services in particular neighbourhoods. The first Sure Start projects were in neighbourhoods of particular need, but Blunkett, Jowell and other ministers were clear that these projects were an experiment they hoped would set in motion a new approach to services. They had learned from the Family Advice Centres and the Home Office Community Development Project of the late 1960s and early 1970s that it was useless to set up demonstration projects and simply hope that everyone would imitate them. Blunkett had also had direct experience of what could go wrong with such an approach in efforts to reorganize the social services department in Sheffield when he was Labour Party leader there.

A new system of regulation

Meeting the Childcare Challenge had said that an improved system of regulation would be critically important to securing better childcare services. A specific issue on which action started quickly was the need to bring some order and clarity to the chaotic jumble of different qualifications. Local authority childcare inspection teams had to make decisions on the relevance of different qualifications (including those secured in other countries) with little to guide them.

This created major headaches. Work, therefore, began on a new qualifications 'framework' in 1999.

The main issue, however, was the regulation of settings registered under Part X of the Children Act and how this should relate to the management of the nursery grant system in England and Wales. In 1998 the Department of Health (which still had oversight of Part X) and the DfEE issued a consultation paper on regulation, asking 39 questions. The document covered a wide range of issues. Few noticed the critical importance of Question 21: 'Should regulation be organised locally or nationally by a body such as Ofsted? Are there other possibilities?' Most of those who did notice it assumed that Ofsted was mentioned as an example of a national regulatory agency. They did not recognize that the government were actually seeing it as the body that could take over. Directors of social services appear to have believed that, if a national body were to be given responsibility, it would be the new Care Commission that the government intended to launch in 2002. They were shocked when it was announced in August 1999 that it had been decided to allocate the task in England to the body responsible for schools inspections.

Several considerations seem to have been behind this decision (which had probably been made even before the consultation took place).

One was that there were frequent differences between local authorities in the conditions of registration they imposed, in their willingness to use powers of enforcement, in their readiness to offer support to providers and in the salaries they offered inspection staff. There was no obvious justification for these inconsistencies to be found in differences between local authority areas. Variation also caused problems when childminders moved from one local authority to another or day care providers ran settings in different parts of the country. A national body in England (with similar arrangements in Wales, Scotland and Northern Ireland) might be expected to bring greater consistency and, therefore, 'territorial justice'.

Another was that Ofsted already controlled the inspection system for settings considered eligible to receive nursery grant payments. It made sense to work towards merging that system with regulation under Part X.

Finally, it was important that the battle inside the government for Education to have the lead role in early childhood services had been won. The social work profession would no longer retain a dominant role. The previous two or three decades had seen growing public concern about child protection. As a result, work with children in the social services departments became focused on that issue with growing intensity. The government agreed the issue was critical. It passed a Protection of Children Act in 1999 and was taking steps to establish a national Criminal Records Bureau to facilitate checks on people who wanted to work with children or vulnerable adults. However, an exclusive focus on child protection had squeezed out of the picture more supportive work with families ('preventive work' as it was often known). This was the reverse of what Seebohm and others had anticipated in 1968. It was especially critical for work on early childhood as about half of the children that came to the attention of child protection services were under the age of 5. Margaret Hodge, who was one of the ministers with responsibility for early childhood, had clashed with social workers over their priorities when she was in local government. Both she and Blunkett appear to have been worried that leaving the regulation of childcare under the control of social workers would impede the development of the broad agenda they had in mind for early years provision.

The immediate response among the leaders of the social work profession to the plan to transfer responsibility to Ofsted was angry, even hysterical (Baldock, 2001: 19). The striking thing about that response is how quickly it faded away. Nothing could have demonstrated more clearly that the social work establishment was not really interested in early childhood operations except, perhaps, as a resource that social workers could deploy for families that were failing but not essentially abusive. The transfer to Ofsted in England (and to the Welsh Assembly Government in that country) was duly incorporated in the Care Standards Act (2000).

The implementation of that part of the Care Standards Act was delayed until after the general election of 2001. As a result it was some time before the advantages of the new system (or the numerous initial difficulties) became clear, but it was possible to discern what the government hoped would be the consequences of the reform.

They sought greater consistency of judgements in relation to registrations, inspections and investigations into alleged failures to adhere to requirements. The fact that consistency was a key objective of the reform makes it all the more surprising that in 2010 Ofsted should have decided to put it at risk by outsourcing inspections to a number of different agencies.

The government wanted less rigid adherence to rules and better professional assessments from childcare inspectors. Local authority teams had varied in the degree of judgement they expected of their childcare inspectors. Some registered and inspected on the basis of very limited criteria relating to those things that could be measured arithmetically ('counting the toilets' as a common phrase had it). Some expected inspectors to analyse more carefully what was happening in settings and to adopt a flexible approach to the application of official standards. This strategy often worked well, but it was not clearly thought through. 'Flexibility' was precisely too flexible a concept to be clear or fair. The new National Standards that were to inform Ofsted's work were an improvement, being based more on outcomes (that is to say, the quality of the experiences of children and their parents) than on 'inputs' (that is to say, the specific measures the provider was supposed to put in place). This was a significant advance. It challenged many of the inspectors who had transferred from local authorities and even some providers. Things had gone too far for some people. This, in combination with protests about the way that childminders were to be exempt from the rules about corporal punishment that applied to group settings, led *Nursery World* to initiate a campaign demanding 'Stop the Drop' (in standards). However, the areas of uncertainty that the new approach opened up had been there for years. Many providers were already unclear about what they should be doing in relation to equal opportunities and cultural diversity. It made life difficult at first when both providers and inspectors were told that more was expected than a written policy or the presence of a wok in the home corner to demonstrate commitment to anti-racism, but this reshaping opened up new opportunities for professional development.

The government wanted to see childcare and nursery education inspections more closely integrated. Many nurseries and playgroups offered both day care and funded early education. It was also possible for childminders to do this if they joined approved networks. Ofsted already had responsibility for nursery grant inspections. The transfer of childcare inspectors to Ofsted created an opportunity for a combined inspection system, reducing waste and the risk of conflict between requirements imposed by the two types of inspector.

The government wanted councils to offer improved support services to both parents and providers of childcare. Under the 1989 Act local authorities had had a duty to regulate childminding and day care, but only permissive powers to undertake other related tasks, including information to parents and advice to registered settings and their providers. The use made of permissive powers varied. Some local authorities simply undertook the minimum amount of regulation work they considered inescapable. Some allowed their childcare inspectors to offer information to parents (directly or through some other agency) and to provide training and other forms of support to people who were registered or applying for registration. Some had two teams of regulation staff – one to deal with registrations and continue to provide support thereafter, the other dealing with inspection, investigation and enforcement. Others again had both a registration and inspection team and a separate team of under-5s advisers who were there to support providers. Section 79V of the Care Standards Act envisaged a total separation of regulation, on the one hand, and information, support and advice on the other. The latter was to become a new duty imposed on local authorities after their childcare inspectors had been transferred. Childcare inspectors from local authority teams that had undertaken both types of work were often unhappy about this separation. In the end it seems to have worked well. It was in those authorities where little use had been made of the earlier permissive powers that most was achieved. They were often able to think more clearly about objectives and the means to achieve them than those that assumed initially that they already knew what needed doing because their staff had been doing it for some time.

The plan to transfer responsibility for regulation may have been the most important change the government made between 1997 and 2001. It was the largest in scale, the one that had the most immediate practical impact and it clarified the direction in which things were moving, in particular, the lead role of Education. Ironically, after it had happened, regulation became less central to policy on early childhood. From the Infant Life Protection Act of 1872 to the 1989 Children Act the regulation of early childhood services had been given greater emphasis than their positive promotion. Changes in regulation regimes may well happen again in the future, but 2001 was probably the last time that such changes would take centre stage.

Outside government and the statutory sector

In 1997 a new approach to early childhood services began to take shape in the National Childcare Strategy, the introduction of nursery grants, the push towards greater coordination of services and the reform of regulation. Things were also moving in the world outside central and local government.

There was continuing growth in the availability of provision and the expectations of parents. The expansion of provision was not always reflected in some of the statistical data. The increase in the number of independent sector day nurseries went alongside a continuing slow decline in local authority provision (both nursery schools and day nurseries) and a more rapid decline in the number of childminders, playgroups and holiday playschemes. Against this there is the fact that the quality of the settings that remained was often better and that many settings were taking on larger numbers of children and a wider range of services (with many pre-schools moving from session to full day care and nurseries providing after-school care).

Outside some playcare activities, the workforce remained overwhelmingly young, female and white. However, the view that men as such could not be trusted to work with children was losing ground and the first steps were being taken to secure a more varied workforce. In particular, there was a greater readiness to consider recruiting people with physical disabilities, something from which many managers of both settings and inspection services had recoiled because of concerns about safety that had been instinctive rather than carefully considered.

Ideas on equality of opportunities and inclusion were taking a stronger hold. The Children Act (1989) had spoken of agencies, including early years settings, needing to take into account the 'religious persuasion, racial origin and cultural and linguistic background' of any child receiving services. This was primarily a consolidation of existing law. When the Act was implemented, the scope of the requirement was broadened in practice by staff dealing with the issue to one of celebrating cultural and other forms of diversity in all settings, not just those taking children from minorities. The period of Blair's first parliament saw the publication of several influential texts dealing with racism in early years settings (Brown, 1998; Lane, 1999, Siraj-Blatchford, 2000). It is a measure of how perspectives were altering that the book published in 1998 spoke of 'combating discrimination' and that published in 2000 of 'supporting identity'.

Another area of practice where progress was being made was appreciation of the outdoors as a resource for learning. Several initiatives took place in Scotland. This reflected a long-standing tradition there. Wilderspin (1840: 270) had noted and approved of the intelligence with which Scottish schools made use of outdoor space. Margaret McMillan was also convinced that the garden was a valuable location for learning. By the 1970s the disappearance of the worst health problems in towns and cities generated a tendency to see any emphasis on the open air in social provision as mere nostalgia for pre-urban society. (Pearson, 1975, Chapter 7 is a good example of this attitude). When Bilton published the first edition of her book on outdoor play in the early years in 1998, she encouraged practitioners to examine the issue more intelligently and to return to the original concept of the nursery school. This coincided with the arrival of reports from other countries, especially in Scandinavia, about their use of outdoor space for learning. Learning Through Landscapes, a voluntary organization that also worked with older children, helped many early childhood settings to develop their practice in this area.

Active use of outdoor space will always be easier if the design of premises is appropriate. When the government decided in 1945 not to go ahead with constructing more nurseries, it discouraged architects from taking an interest in buildings intended for children. In the 1990s most settings were in buildings that had been designed with other uses in mind or in boxes where children could be contained safely, but which did nothing to help staff to meet their other needs. Building design is not everything. Some of the best playgroups I have encountered were housed in dingy, barn-like church buildings constructed before the First World War. However, good design does facilitate good practice. The basic building template for its new nurseries commissioned by Nord Anglia and the carefully considered design adopted by Virgin Active sports centres for their crèches were examples of what might be done. A start had been made, although it was only a start.

Another issue to which closer attention was paid was that of the cognitive development of babies. For a long time it was assumed that babies needed nothing but good physical care until they were speaking fluently and could engage with adults in word-based learning. As just one consequence, nappy-changing in settings with large numbers of babies could be conducted with sound attention to hygiene, but a brutal disregard of the children's feelings. The basis for better appreciation of child development had been established by theoretical work on child psychology and later on emotional development in the period from the 1890s to the immediate post-war period. As the twentieth century ended, more sophisticated experiments in child psychology and the invention of relevant equipment, such as the geodesic net, opened up the possibility of much closer examination of the cognitive and emotional development of the pre-verbal child. The book by the Americans Gopnik, Meltzoff and Kuhl, first published in the UK in 1999, drew attention to what was happening in this field. It gave theoretical underpinning to the ideas that some had developed through their practice. The period after 2001 was to see closer attention being paid to all the needs of the youngest children than ever before.

The final alteration that can be mentioned is the growing use of new technology, something about which Blair was enthusiastic, as he was about more or less anything with the word 'new' in its name. New technology (ICT) had two consequences for the development of early childhood provision. One was that a different medium of debate and consultation had been created. The government made some use of it before 2001, much greater use afterwards, as it became increasingly common for people to have personal computers at home and access to the Internet. The other was that a new set of educational tools became available, although it was a while before practitioners began to catch up with this. The fact that the workforce was an unusually young one was probably an advantage in this respect.

Devolution

The final aspect of the period that should be considered is the decision to give a degree of political autonomy to the major parts of the UK outside England. Thatcher had been hostile to devolution, something she feared would lead to the break-up of the United Kingdom. Blair introduced legislation to create new forms of government in Wales and Scotland and pursued negotiations in Northern Ireland in the hope of establishing a new form of devolved government there. Early childhood services provided a sphere in which the devolved regimes could demonstrate an ability to innovate with energy and purpose. Wales, Scotland and Northern Ireland all developed their own approaches to policy on early childhood (Clark and Waller, 2007). Children in those countries benefited. These efforts also helped to enliven debate on the kind of services that were needed across the UK. This had an impact on England in the longer run, making it easier to win the case for a post of Children's Commissioner and revise the Foundation Stage guidance (Baldock et al., 2009, Chapter 5).

Conclusion

In 2001 many of those who had been pressing for reform of early childhood services were disappointed at the slow rate of progress. The advocates of change within the government would probably have defended themselves by arguing that things could not have gone much more quickly. They appeared to take it for granted that there was too much conservatism about this issue in the social work and teaching professions and among the public in general. It was after the general election of 2001 that the pace began to quicken.

Exercise

Read *Meeting the Childcare Challenge*. How far have the objectives outlined in that document been realized? In what ways have things taken a direction that its authors may not have intended? Consider the reasons why this may have happened.

Further reading

Only a few years after he left office there is a massive literature on Blair's time as prime minister. However, little or no attention is paid in those publications to the issues with which this book is concerned. Even other aspects of social policy receive less space than his foreign policy or his style of political leadership. This makes it difficult to recommend further reading for the period. Jenkins (2007) is, again, a useful source on the general political background.

6   The government's policy on early childhood takes shape (2001–2007)

The period between the elections of 1997 and 2001 saw important innovations in early childhood policy. When the Labour Party secured a second term of office it was still unclear whether things would go much further.

This chapter describes:

- some of the developments that took place immediately after the general election of 2001;
- the publication and impact of *Every Child Matters*;
- the difficulties that began to emerge with the National Childcare Strategy;
- the debate about Sure Start's contribution to combating poverty;
- the uncertainties about early childhood policy that remained towards the end of Blair's time as prime minister.

Introduction

Blair and others had been astounded by the size of the majority he secured in 1997. When he won the next election in 2001 it was with a reduced majority, but still a comfortable one. TV satirists spoke as though the Conservative Party was dead and buried. The Liberal Democrats had not made the kind of breakthrough that offered them any prospect of gaining power. Secure in power, at least for the time being, Blair and his colleagues had every reason to moderate the caution they had displayed in office so far.

Then came the attacks of September 11th 2001 in America. The aftermath was to dominate the rest of Blair's time at Number 10. He began to see himself as a key figure in the 'War Against Terrorism'. His outlook on that issue was never repudiated by his party, even after he left office, but he failed to take a large part of the country with him and his contentious foreign policy was at the very least a distraction from social policy.

Even if events and his bid for a place in world history had not interfered, it is far from clear that Blair would have seen work on early childhood services as significant. Apart from the NHS, which forced itself upon his attention, his main priority in social policy was education and, as was explained in the previous chapter, he valued early childhood services less as an aspect of education than as a means of getting unemployed parents back to work. In February 2002, less than a year after the election, Estelle Morris, the new Education Secretary, told the House of Commons that early childhood was no longer a key issue for her department, which would now be turning its attention to secondary schools (Tweed, 2002). She was forced by some of the responses to backtrack a little, but her statement showed how the government was thinking.

Problems with the childcare strategy

Investment in childcare was not proving to be the quick fix for welfare dependency Blair had hoped it would be. Many lone mothers remained unconvinced that their children would be better off if they went out to jobs that were financially and psychologically unrewarding (Prideaux, 2005: 137–8). One study showed that, even with help towards childcare costs, many parents remained worse off financially if they returned to work (Evans, 2003). Of course, the help that had become available with childcare persuaded some parents to return to work when taken in conjunction with other reasons for doing so. That was not enough, even before the later recession, to generate a mass transfer 'from welfare to workfare'. A report by the economists at PriceWaterhouseCoopers suggested that the only way out of the dilemma was universal childcare for children under 5 (Ambler et al., 2003). That was not on Blair's agenda. Even Blunkett had discounted it as unrealistic and unaffordable.

In the period 1997–2001 the government had introduced changes that had not been put fully into effect by the time of the election. Work on this was a significant aspect of the period that immediately followed.

Establishing Ofsted's Early Years Directorate

One example was the launch of Ofsted's Early Years Directorate in the autumn of 2001. No one should have expected this to be easy. Considerable effort had been put into the preparation and Maggie Smith, the first head of service, was a popular choice among early years practitioners. Nevertheless, the undertaking was on a large scale and there were bound to be initial hiccups. Some of these were relatively easy to tackle. Ofsted had planned unannounced inspections before realizing that it would not be possible for inspectors to turn up unannounced at military bases and demand immediate access to their childcare facilities – especially at a time of armed conflict. Others took longer to resolve. Ofsted's software for the new regulatory system needed significant revision almost immediately. The Criminal Records Bureau, which came into operation in 2002, was designed on the basis of an unrealistically low estimate of the number of checks that would be required. The Early Years Directorate was also damaged by the widespread view that its regulations entailed a drop in the standards expected of services.

Nevertheless, progress was made. The process of re-registering providers under the new legislation was completed and the first steps were taken towards integrating care and education inspections. There were suggestions that Ofsted should extend its role still further and undertake some regulation, however minimal, of nannies and of playcare schemes for children over 7. The first of these proposals ran up against fears of excessive interference in private family life, especially the family life of more affluent and articulate people. It was still rumbling on some years later. The second raised the issue of whether there is a significant 'care' aspect to those agencies that offer children training in specific sporting or artistic skills (football training schemes, schools of dance, etc.). The government was reluctant to address the issue because of the potential costs of additional inspections and because of the complications caused by the fact that the distinction between care and education was deeply embedded in the relevant laws.

The new responsibilities of local authorities

The new services offering support to parents and providers that the local authorities were required to put in place by September 2001 also got under way. Children's information services were set up across England. Providers were given more consistent support with registration applications and the outcome of inspections. The experience of the Early Years Development and Childcare Partnerships was rather more mixed. Some EYDCPs had difficulty securing full participation by social services departments and community health services. Hardly any of them secured effective representation of parents. Some really did begin to develop local strategies. Many were simply instruments for consultation of 'stakeholders' by the education departments and their performance in that limited respect was varied.

Changes in the curriculum that had started before the election were important. The Foundation Stage guidance became an established aspect of life for many providers. In 2002 this was supplemented by a document on work with younger children – *Birth to Three Matters* (Abbott, 2002). This gave official backing to the kind of approaches for which Goldschmied and Jackson (1994) and others had argued and which had been adopted in the best settings. It was widely distributed to practitioners, support workers and childcare inspectors and was the subject of a series of articles in *Nursery World*. It was simply advice and had no basis in statute. Nevertheless, it buried the old belief that babies needed little more than adequate physical care and laid the foundation for the changes in curriculum guidance that were to happen a few years later. Other developments that took place were the replacement of 'baseline assessment' in schools by the new Foundation Stage profiles and the decision to impose the Special Educational Needs Code of Practice on pre-school settings receiving nursery grants – two small but significant reforms. By the start of 2002 the government was edging its way towards a more comprehensive approach to early education.

Changes outside England

The constitutional changes that had taken place in Wales and Scotland also had consequences for early childhood. Wales was the first part of the United Kingdom to appoint a Children's Commissioner. In fact, the idea had been raised there while Thatcher was Prime Minister, but had been dismissed by her. The Welsh Assembly Government's *Plan for Wales*, which dealt with a range of social policy issues, highlighted childcare and set a number of targets. In Scotland the Executive (as the Scottish Government was called at the time) set out a programme for improving children's services that prioritized closer coordination. In Northern Ireland a new 'enriched curriculum' for younger children was piloted. Early years theorists in England were already accustomed to making critical comparisons between provision in their own country and in some other parts of Europe. They now began to invoke developments in other parts of the UK as evidence of what could be done (National Children's Homes, 2003; Baldock et al., 2009: 92).

Beyond the consolidation of earlier initiatives

Other changes took place in the second half of 2001 and during 2002 that went beyond the implementation and consolidation of the period after 1997.

The most important of these was the creation of a single Sure Start Unit as part of the Department for Education and Skills, bringing together the separate teams that had existed beforehand and edging towards a more inte-grated service. Sure Start, which had been the name used for a number of specially funded projects in particular localities, soon became the name of the government's entire early childhood programme (Sure Start Unit, 2003).

Policies outside central and local government included the development of quality assurance schemes for early childhood services and the creation of a number of large 'chains' of providers, securing for their individual settings economies of scale in fields such as recruitment, in-house training and building design.

Things appeared to be moving forward at a steady, if unexciting, pace. A review initiated by the government spoke of progress, although it also identified difficulties, for example, with the effectiveness of EYDCPs (Strategy Unit, 2002). The impression of progress made it possible for Estelle Morris to speak of early childcare as though everything was basically sorted. The response to the death of just one child altered the picture drastically.

The Laming Report (2003)

In February 2000 Victoria Climbié, a child living in London with her great-aunt and her great-aunt's partner, died as a result of the abuse she suffered at their hands. Nearly a year later her carers were found guilty of murder. In April 2001 Lord Laming, an experienced social worker, was asked to set up an inquiry into what had happened. All this took place before the election of 2001, but his inquiry was an exhaustive one and the results were not published until nearly two years later (Laming, 2003).

It was not at first evident that it would have any greater impact on early childhood services than many similar inquiries that had taken place since the death of Maria Colwell. Victoria's injuries were particularly horrific and Laming's report was much more specific and organizationally radical in its recommendations than others had been. However, his main proposals were around the theme of closer cooperation and better information-sharing between agencies. Similar things had often been said in the past. He barely picked up on the fact that in this case, as in many others, the lack of direct contact between the child and the investigating social workers and other professionals was a crucial factor in the situation leading to her death.

It had long been a weakness of child protection social work that the staff did not necessarily possess skills in talking and, more important, listening to children, especially very young children. Of course, many were very capable in that respect, but this was because of their own personalities and experience rather than because their training and supervision had nurtured those abilities. It is easier to make specific recommendations on administrative matters, such as information sharing and the structures to support it, than to work out ways of fostering professional development in an aspect of the work that has been allowed to remain neglected. The Laming Report led to reforms in child protection, but its attention to information sharing may have created as many difficulties as it has solved. An excess of information, not to mention the time spent on recording it in the first instance, can make it difficult for professional workers to spot the salient features of a particular situation.

However one evaluates the outcomes for child protection of the Laming Report, it is still unclear why it also led to significant changes in other aspects of government policy on children, young children in particular. Two things may have determined the nature of the response.

One was that public outrage about the case underlined the fact that an exclusive focus on secondary schools (and on teenagers in general) might allow other problems to develop. The case may have been one specifically of child abuse; it raised general questions about children's welfare.

The other was that since the proposal to transfer regulation of day care and childminding to Ofsted the social work profession had been nervous that child protection would fall off the government's agenda. An approach to child welfare that connected child protection with a wider range of services in a very clear way was a response to that particular source of criticism. If that was the idea, it appeared to have backfired when the Conservatives in opposition called before the 2010 election for an end to the legislation obliging local authorities in England to establish children's trusts on the grounds that the trusts had made no significant difference to the effectiveness of arrangements for safe-guarding, whatever else they might have achieved.

Developing the concept of partnership

The government announced the next phase of its policy for children in September 2003 (DfES, 2003). Before that happened, several steps were taken that indicated the direction that was being adopted.

The inter-departmental review of 2002 had concluded that only about one-fifth of EYDCPs were working well. Even those that did operate effectively faced the fundamental difficulty that they did not have final control of funding allocated for childcare. They were just not constituted in a way that would have made this possible. Some argued that there should have been more clarity over the status and functions of the EYDCPs. The government was ready to agree, but did not draw the conclusion that reform was feasible. There were other solutions to consider. The inter-departmental review was said to be just a review and not a policy statement, but English local authorities got the message and began to invest less in the partnerships. They stumbled forward for a while, but many went out of existence in 2004.

The government remained committed to the concept of 'partnership' itself as a key aspect of 'the third way', but wanted to develop the kind of work that had been done in the more successful EYDCPs in wider partnership struc-tures. Building on the Local Government Act (2000) it launched a system of 'Local Area Agreements', the first 20 of which had been completed by the time of the general election in 2005. These agreements represented an attempt to secure cooperation between Whitehall and local authorities on objectives for the areas the authorities served, with the main thrust of the agenda being set as always by central government. Formal partnerships were constructed to take programmes of local development forward. There was space for variation, but eventually it became usual for local authorities in England to have a Partnership Board for Children and Young People.

However ineffective most EYDCPs had been, early childhood services lost out in this change because of the following:

- The voluntary and community sector is too variegated to have a strong centralized voice in any town, city or rural area and this makes it difficult for its representatives to hold their own against those of the large statutory bodies.
- Children and young people's partnerships have paid particular attention to teenagers, partly because of government priorities, partly because of public concern about young people and partly because young people themselves have become more organized and articulate in explaining what they see as their needs. Agencies working with primary school and pre-school children have lost out as a result.
- The small, but significant, private sector in early childhood provision has rarely had a voice at all in the children's partnerships. Major commercial and industrial interests have been influential in over-arching partnership structures, but they have usually been concerned with macro-economic development. The concerns of young children have appeared very rarely on their agendas.
- The disappearance of most EYDCPs meant that opportunities were lost for dialogue between schools, on the one hand, and private and voluntary day care settings on the other. Such dialogue was never easy, but it had been vital as a way of avoiding conflict. Some local authorities have established coordinating mechanisms for children's services working in sub-divisions of their areas, sometimes called 'service districts'. These experiments, like the authority-wide partnerships, have usually been focused on children in general rather than early childhood and have not always met with success.

These consequences did not become fully apparent until later, but the signs were there in the summer of 2003.

The government also considered the coordination of services at a neighbourhood level or at least at the level of clusters of neighbourhoods. A number of government-funded projects – early excellence centres, settings established as part of the Neighbourhood Nurseries Initiative and the Sure Start local projects – were already in operation. In March 2003 the government issued details of a plan to have at least one 'children's centre' in every local authority ward in England, with the first batch to be established in the poorest wards in the country. Although the earlier local projects constituted a starting point for this programme, children's centres were intended to be mechanisms for the local coordination of services – a new way of organizing services rather than just additional settings.

Making every child matter

The publication of Lord Laming's report on Victoria Climbié prompted the government to develop a more ambitious strategy for children. The Green Paper *Every Child Matters* (DES, 2003) proposed a set of criteria under which all services for children and young people were to be judged – the five outcomes for children it should be possible to expect. In early childhood services this had some success in forcing people to re-evaluate what they were doing. It also provided a formula that could be rolled out whenever it was required without necessarily being given all that much thought. It is, perhaps, still too soon to determine whether this has led to more effective action or just another formula for pious pronouncements.

The five outcomes

The aim of the Every Child Matters programme is to give all children the support they need to

be healthy
stay safe
enjoy and achieve
make a positive contribution
achieve economic well-being.

This means that the organisations involved with providing services to children – from hospitals and schools to police and voluntary groups – will be learning in new ways, sharing information and working together to protect children and young people from harm and help them to achieve what they want in life. Children and young people will have far more say about issues that affect them as individuals and collectively.

Source: http://www.dcsf,gov.uk.everychildmatters/
about/aims (accessed 25/5/10)

Many of the proposals in the Green Paper were given legislative force in the Children Act (2004) and there were specific provisions made for early childhood services in the Childcare Act (2006). A multiplicity of initiatives followed directly from the legislation or were influenced by the Green Paper. These included:

- the establishment of new Safeguarding Boards;
- a new system of Children's Trusts;
- an extended role for Ofsted, so that it became the inspection body for most children's services;
- the production of a new curriculum for the Foundation Stage, one that would also cover children under 3;
- the launch of a Children's Workforce Development Council.

There were also some tentative moves towards the creation of the kind of single early years profession Moss and others had been advocating – in particular, the new Early Years Professional Status. Other initiatives that related to early child-hood services were:

- reforms in the systems intended to offer parents financial assistance with childcare;
- the publication of a ten-year plan for the development of childcare;
- the continued roll-out of children's centres.

More was now expected, but, with the raising of the stakes, difficulties became apparent.

The continuing weakness of the childcare strategy

Local authorities had been given responsibility for facilitating the universal availability of childcare, but they were not to do this by providing direct services. When Vevers (2005) interviewed key people in several local authorities, he found them uncertain about the precise implications of this. At the very least this led to variation between local authorities in the way they interpreted the task they had been set.

One issue that became increasingly problematic was that of 'extended' schools. The government had been interested in this concept since 1997 and in 2001 had published a White Paper that outlined its plans for primary schools, including extensions of their role (DES, 2001). In March 2003 Cathy Ashton, the Minister for Sure Start, announced a funding package for schools offering a range of services to young children with the target of having at least one school in each local authority area in England 'extended' in this way by 2006. In October of that year, Hodge, the Minister for Children, spoke of the success of the extended schools programme to date and of plans to create a national support service for them delivered by a company called ContinYou. A government-sponsored research team was enthusiastic about the work already being undertaken (National Foundation for Education Research, 2003). Others had anxieties that extended schools presented yet another threat to the sustainability of independent settings and stoked up the tensions between different sectors. In addition, one of Blair's favourite projects helped to undermine expansion in the number of extended schools. He wanted to promote independent 'academies' that would replace schools in the maintained sector that were deemed to be failing. In 2005 plans were issued for an increase in the number of these academies. It was far from clear that academies would be happy to be 'extended', given the additional expenditure entailed. This complication and other factors led to a situation by the middle of 2006 where the available statistics suggested that the government would fail to meet its target of all schools having extended services by 2010 and would do so by a long way.

Another problematic aspect of the childcare strategy was the contribution the government expected of employers. The idea that they should be willing to meet at least part of the childcare costs of their employees as one of their own essential running costs had been around since the 1940s. It reflected the ideas of some of the more imaginative employers in the nineteenth century. The most positive response in recent years had been from public service employers. In the 1990s a large number of civil service departments and organizations such as the BBC had contracted with various providers to offer subsidized nursery and holiday playcare to their employees. Child Care Enterprise Ltd, a not-for-profit company based on Tyneside, secured many of these deals. The National Health Service had its own major programme for developing childcare for its staff. With a few exceptions private companies invested less in workplace childcare. In 2005 Brown, as Chancellor, created new tax relief measures to assist employer-supported childcare. The growth he may have expected never materialized. It emerged that the government scheme could actually have an adverse impact on the tax position of some parents. There was also uncertainty about the types of childcare that could draw down tax concessions. The development of workplace nurseries in the public sector did not just slow down, it went into reverse. By early in 2007 the BBC and several civil service departments had closed down the contracts they had had with providers of workplace-related settings.

Sure Start and the question of poverty

Blair had made it clear in 1996 that he was more interested in childcare as part of the solution to the problem of welfare dependency than as something that directly benefited children. Childcare was to make life better for them by adding to their parents' ability to increase their incomes. It was often assumed by commentators that the local Sure Start projects (and some earlier funding initiatives for settings in deprived areas) were designed to tackle child poverty. It is not clear why this was so. Other aspects of government policy – the New Deal on jobs and the tax credit system – were far more central to that objective. Unless it was assumed that poverty had no source in the economic structures of the country, it should have been evident that the projects could offer no solution to poverty as such. At best they could help some families escape it. Moreover, research evidence was emerging that children could be disadvantaged if they were in settings where a large number of families were on low incomes (Vevers, 2003). As the first Sure Start projects were sited in the poorest areas, that factor was bound to affect their work. To make matters worse, the freedom allowed to local projects to experiment with various types of activity rendered any evaluation conducted within a few years of the programme starting inevitably problematic.

Blunkett had been quite clear that he did not intend Sure Start to be a programme solely for the disadvantaged. Others, including some of Blair's closest allies in the party, agreed. Stephen Byers argued that Sure Start programme should move as soon as possible from one focused on the poorest areas to one of universal application (Thomson, 2004). In spite of that the assumption that they were the Labour Party's answer to child poverty persisted. In fact, as the programme settled down, evidence began to emerge that the local projects might not solve the problem of child poverty, but they could have some modest impact on it (Gaunt, 2006a). This came from work by Professor Edward Melhuish, the man whose earlier research (National Evaluation of Sure Start Research Team, 2005) had identified some of the initial difficulties of the earlier local projects.

As the expansion of children's centres continued, even more problems began to emerge. Children's centres had been proposed as mechanisms for coordinating the work of different agencies – a new way of organizing services rather than a new type of service. However, because the word 'centre' was used, local plans were often devised in terms of specific buildings (new or improved) rather than networks.

In some areas there was less involvement on the part of community health staff than the government had wanted.

A report by the National Audit Office early in 2007 cast doubt on the government's ability to maintain the roll-out of children's centres, not just because of inadequate funding, but also because of a lack of trained personnel and other resources.

Signs of malaise

In this context it was hardly surprising that early childhood services, which had appeared to be on the brink of a transformation of some kind in the years 2001–03, developed signs of serious malaise.

The number of childminders continued to diminish across England, although it was arguable that the service of those who remained was of higher quality. The greatest loss, although not necessarily the most significant in terms of the mere number of places, was the continuing decline in the number of nursery schools. The bright hopes of the late 1930s were finally being destroyed. Nursery schools might have provided some of the best focal points for the new children's centres if they had been supported. The overriding tendency was for local authorities to ditch them, seeing them as settings less able to offer value for money than extended primary schools. There was nothing inevitable about this. In June 2002 Ashton had told the Forum for Maintained Nursery Schools that they should be at the heart of the government's initiatives on early childhood (Mercer, 2002). They believed her and in 2005 issued guidance to nursery schools on coping with the transition to children's centres. This failed to impress most local authorities. They continued to regard nursery schools as a type of service that was now redundant.

The most worrying symptom of what was happening was the discontent among staff in local authority day nurseries – one group that might have been expected to flourish when childcare was being promoted. The more capable and ambitious individuals among them were able to use the early years units in local authorities to secure the kind of managerial positions they would never have attained in the social services departments in the 1970s or 1980s. Most did less well out of the changes taking place. There were strikes by nursery nurses in several places, especially in 2003 and 2004. In 2007, as new pay structures started to come into full operation under the 'single status agreements', nursery nurses were often faced with serious threats to their incomes. Human resources teams and councillors often chose to regard the care of pre-school children as relatively unskilled work with which any nice young girl could cope quite adequately and to devise new pay scales accordingly.

Critical evaluations of government policy and performance

Against this background there was continued critical evaluation of the gap between the government's stated ambitions and what was actually happening.

Penn and Moss had been voicing such criticisms long before 1997. New voices with similar messages were being heard, among them that of the Centre for Research in Early Childhood at University College in Worcester (Pascal and Bertram, 2006). The government's enthusiastic reception of the report by Rose (2006) on the use of phonics in primary education sparked new criticism because of fears that this would lead eventually to inappropriate teaching styles in pre-schools.

At the same time the wider public were expressing concern about what was happening to all children, not just the youngest. Children in the UK were described as being among the most unhappy and deprived in Europe (Gaunt, 2006b). The media picked up the phrase 'toxic childhood', invented by the educationist Sue Palmer (2006), and employed it lavishly.

There were also voices raising older concerns about the benefits of care outside the family home for young children. In 2004 a BBC TV documentary *Nurseries Undercover* performed a valuable service in showing what could go wrong in badly run settings, but (like the Jacksons' research on childminding a quarter of a century earlier) left many with a nasty impression of all nursery care. This was reinforced by research publications that once again raised fundamental issues about the value of childcare, whatever the quality. Biddulph (2006) questioned whether children under 3 should be in nursery at all. In 2007 Professor Belsky, who had published similar material in the 1980s, was one of a team of researchers in the USA that was critical of the impact of day care on the emotional development of children (Belsky et al. 2007). Their report received remarkably wide attention in Britain for a piece of academic research about another country.

The departure of Tony Blair

Most early years practitioners were too absorbed in their daily tasks to pay very much attention to this kind of debate except where there was a direct impact on them (for example, when many parents became alarmed about their children's nurseries because of publicity given to instances of low quality care). It was important to those making and implementing policy. Blair entered the debate a year after winning the 2005 election. Launching his 'Let's Talk' programme, which was intended to create a new dialogue between government and the governed, he listed Sure Start among a number of statutory services he believed were working less effectively than they might for disadvantaged families (Wintour, 2006). He offered no clarification on what he intended to do about it and events overtook any plans he might have been forming. In 2007, bowing to pressure from within his own party and the public in general, he resigned as prime minister and his Chancellor Gordon Brown took over.

Exercise

Read a copy of *Every Child Matters*. You may well have read it before, but try re-reading it carefully. Does it seem to you an adequate summary of what an overall policy for children should be? Are all the five outcomes relevant to young children? How well do you think the government had done by 2007 in attaining the five outcomes? Where had most been achieved? Where had the least been achieved? If you were asked to compose a document with a similar purpose today, what would be the principal changes you would make to what was said in 2003?

Further reading

Clark and Waller (2007) provide a survey of policy towards the end of the period and one that has the advantage of giving full coverage to developments outside England, not just in Scotland, Wales and Northern Ireland, but also in another member of the European Union – the Irish Republic.

7 The transformation of early childhood services falters (2007–2010)

In the three years that Gordon Brown was prime minister an attempt was made to speed up the transformation of early childhood services. The progress made remained slow and the situation changed with the formation of David Cameron's coalition government in 2010.

This chapter describes:

- the attempt to strengthen early childhood provision;
- changes to the Foundation Stage in England;
- the continuing controversy about Sure Start;
- the revival of interest in informal childcare;
- developments in Scotland, Wales and Northern Ireland;
- debate about early childhood services in the period leading up to the general election of 2010;
- the implications of the outcome of the 2010 election for the immediate future of early childhood services.

Introduction

If it was true that Brown was more enthusiastic about Sure Start than his predecessor had been, his premiership offered an opportunity to build on what had already been done and transform early childhood services in England. (By this stage the other major parts of the United Kingdom had assumed full responsibility for work with children and were busy with the implementation of their own reforms.) One of Brown's first ministerial appointments implied that further progress might be made. The old Department for Education and Employment was split into two, one dealing with tertiary education and vocational training, the other with children, schools and families. This latter department assumed responsibility for Sure Start. Its creation underlined the importance Brown ascribed to the establishment of children's services departments in English local authorities. The restructuring in Whitehall paralleled that earlier development. It was also significant that Brown gave the post of Secretary of State for Children, Schools and Families to Ed Balls, one of his closest colleagues within the party. Balls himself allowed those parts of his portfolio other than schools a high profile in the first few speeches he made after starting in his new post. The government attempted to secure support for the new sense of direction by the publication of the Children's Plan (DCSF, 2007) and a review two years later of progress on the 2004 Ten Year Strategy document (DCSF, 2009).

However, Brown's premiership was weighed down by several difficulties. From Balfour at the beginning of the twentieth century to Callaghan towards its end, those who took over as prime minister after someone else had held the office for a long time found success elusive. There is nothing inevitable in history, but Brown's defeat in 2010 came close. He lacked his predecessor's skills at public relations. Economic problems placed in question all investment in public services, let alone more recent ventures such as Sure Start. A scandal over MPs' expenses cast a shadow on all politicians and their parties, but fed vague feelings that change was desirable that were unhelpful to the government in power.

Strengthening the organizational infrastructure

In August 2007 the old Sure Start grant was replaced by a new £4bn funding package that was intended to make it possible to reach a target of 3 500 Sure Start children's centres by March 2011.

In November 2009 the Apprentices, Skills, Children and Learning Act was passed. As the title suggests, this piece of legislation covered an assortment of topics. Among other things, it provided a firmer legislative base for children's centres and revised some of the existing arrangements for the new safeguarding boards. The duties imposed on local authorities in relation to children's centres allowed a measure of flexibility (speaking of 'sufficient provision to meet local need') that was probably essential in view of the likely impact of the economic crisis on their incomes. Many of the centres were already dropping childcare provision from their services and turning to other activities.

The Act also provided a legislative basis for Children's Trusts and spelled out some of the ways in which they should be organized. In effect, most existing partnerships for children and young people amended their structures to meet the new requirements for trusts. Under earlier arrangements there had been an increase in communication between local authorities and primary care trusts on what each was planning for children. This was better than the near rivalry that often existed before *Every Child Matters*. It left intact many limits to cooperation, especially in the operation of children's centres (Evans, 2009). How far the new Children's Trusts could provide the basis for improved cooperation was a matter of guesswork.

There were other areas where the organizational infrastructure underwent further change.

Ofsted developed its practice of closer concentration on providers that were doing badly, with inspections of successful settings being held at longer intervals. This represented a further widening of the gulf between regulation and support that had started in England in 2001. There were also plans to outsource inspection work to a small number of private companies. The principal one was Tribal, which was also given a major role in relation to residential childcare.

The national Children's Workforce Development Council (CWDC) continued its work on closer integration of the professions involved in work with children, including early childhood services. Its time was spent primarily on information gathering, a priority that left most practitioners only dimly aware of the potential significance of what it was doing. The CWDC took steps that went a little way towards creating a unified early years profession, but not very far. The main obstacles remained the fear among the teaching unions that educational services would be 'diluted' with less qualified staff taking over tasks once reserved for teachers, and the problems of achieving closer integration of work by community nursing staff with that of those involved in early care and education. The latter obstacle was especially problematic because, apart from health visitors, community health personnel rarely worked only with children, let alone the youngest children.

Work continued on the new safeguarding systems created on the basis of the legislation that followed the Laming Report. There were difficulties with public opinion. The media were fairly hostile to the new Vetting and Barring Scheme, often seeing it as another example of government interference where it was not needed. On the other hand, the murder of Baby P in London and a case in Doncaster of two young boys who seriously assaulted other children attracted widespread outrage at the failure of the relevant services to prevent what happened. David Cameron, the leader of the Conservative Party, reflected both these attitudes in speeches that were only a few weeks apart, apparently unaware of any contradiction in what he was saying. There was nothing unusual in critics demanding simultaneously a relaxation of regulations intended to safeguard children and explanations as to why drastic action had not been taken in specific cases. As in earlier years, the well-publicized cases of long drawn-out suffering ending in the deaths of children engendered an ill-informed assumption that it is always easy to distinguish those families that pose a potentially fatal threat to their own children.

The new Early Years Foundation Stage

It was decided to combine the guidance on the Foundation Stage issued in 2000 with the guidance in *Birth to Three Matters*. As well as integrating the two earlier sets of advice, the new guidance made a slight dent in the division between the Foundation Stage and Key Stage 1, since a child could still be treated as belonging to the Foundation Stage shortly before her sixth birthday. This did not amount to a reversal of the decision of 1870 on the point at which formal schooling should begin. It did not even go as far as the parallel guidance in Wales in that respect. It was, however, a shuffling move in that direction.

For that reason and because a particularly well-considered effort was put into preparing practitioners for its implementation, the government probably anticipated a warmer welcome from the relevant professions than the new curriculum received. Playcare workers were concerned about the potential impact on their work. (Some of them were already busy resisting demands from headteachers to convert their out-of-school clubs into something more like homework clubs.) Childminders who had not been in one of the old 'approved networks' for nursery grant purposes were often unhappy about what they saw as new obligations. A campaign group called Open EYE, led by Margaret Edgington and others, argued that the new guidance would lead to pre-school education becoming too formal. It was a matter for debate how far their concerns were justified by the guidance itself or whether they were merely frightened of what some settings would make of it. Certainly, the ways that local authorities looked at the 'Foundation Stage profiles' of children in their areas, the concerns of many KS1 teachers about the 'school readiness' of their children and the impact the endorsement of the phonics approach in schools had on pre-school settings all tended to drive nurseries in the direction of more formal methods than were strictly required by the guidance itself.

Funding

The Labour Party had made more funding available for early childhood services in England and this was important to both parents and providers. However, the funding system was complex for all concerned, entailing as it did several different arrangements – grants for nursery education, vouchers for childcare, working tax credits and different funding streams for financing specific local projects. Well before June 2007 there had been criticisms of how it was working. One major difficulty was that local authorities, who were responsible for deciding the distribution of money between their maintained sector and other providers, were, quite naturally, more sensitive to the funding needs of their own services than they were to those of others. Many settings suffered from the way that some parents took unfair advantage of the system, claiming government money on the basis of arrangements made with providers from whom they withdrew once the money was in their pockets. On the other hand, there were parents who fell innocently into over-claiming on tax credits and faced significant bills when the over-payments were reclaimed.

In October 2007 the Day Care Trust published a report in association with the National Centre for Social Research in which they alleged that the government's strategy had not led to any significant increase in the use of registered childcare by working parents. They said the system was complex, but still failed to take into account changes in working patterns. For example, 87 per cent of households now included at least one person whose working hours were 'untypical', i.e. were not confined to 9am–5pm Monday to Friday. The way that day care services were provided often failed to take this development into account.

A report commissioned by the government itself published in 2007 was also critical. HEDRA Consulting, the company that undertook the research, concluded that existing funding of nursery education was failing to meet the hourly fees in some parts of the country and that, as a consequence, the government's planned increase of time funded to fifteen hours a week would lead to difficulties. They also noted that some nursery education providers were receiving more in funding than the actual costs of their education services, while others, especially in the South of England, had higher costs than the money they received. Moreover, most of those that appeared to be making a profit on nursery education were using it, at least partly, to reduce the fees they charged parents for children under 3 rather than simply to make more profit.

Discontent about the nursery education grant system rumbled on, fuelled by information on the DCSF's own website that illustrated just how much variation there was between local authorities in the way they dealt with the independent sector in this respect. By 2010 many private providers were thinking of pulling out of the system before the date arrived when they were expected to increase the number of education hours to fifteen a week, but had not reached a final conclusion. It was just too difficult for them to tell whether they stood to lose more money by staying in the scheme or leaving it.

The funding arrangements for childcare were also proving problematic. A proposal from the think tank Policy Exchange (Hakim et al., 2008) to replace the existing system by what they called a parental care allowance of £50 a week had a mixed response. It would have simplified administration considerably and given parents greater choice as to whether to go out to work or stay at home with their children, but it meant abandoning one of the foundation stones of the Labour Party's policy on childcare. This was not likely to happen. On the other hand, an online survey conducted by Mumsnet demonstrated growing demands for funding to take a form that would support parents who chose to stay at home with their children (Defries, 2010b).

The Day Care Trust warned that the costs of childcare were continuing to rise without very obvious gains to providers or their staff. They were especially concerned about the situation in after-school settings, which were more vulnerable to the consequences of an economic downturn than full day care or even sessional pre-schools (Day Care Trust, 2009). The problem of rising costs was partially obscured by the fact that many parents who used such services were among the more affluent. However, if accessible and affordable childcare was to be an element in government strategy on reducing child poverty, the signs were that things were getting worse rather than better.

They had two ways of dealing with this issue. One was to scrap the tax relief on childcare vouchers on the grounds that the more affluent benefited from them disproportionately. Public protest forced them to back off. The other was to take forward plans for a single funding formula. This also met opposition. Local authorities and teaching unions expressed concern that the formula would hit the maintained sector, in particular the income of the remaining nursery schools. A Select Committee Inquiry was set up in the House of Commons and full implementation was delayed until April 2011, i.e. after the forthcoming general election.

Childcare and child poverty

The annual surveys conducted on behalf of the Joseph Rowntree Foundation showed that child poverty was increasing in those households where at least one adult was working (MacInnes et al., 2009). It also appeared that it was growing at a faster rate in the more affluent parts of England (Hirsch, 2009). Both these results were in some ways counter-intuitive and demonstrated that the problems were more fundamental than Blair and his colleagues had been prepared to recognize in 1997. There was also worrying evidence from research commissioned by the government itself that low-income families continued to distrust professional childcare (DCSF and Department for Business, Innovation and Skills, 2009; National Centre for Social Research, 2010). This was not helped by the fact that the settings that were of the lowest quality according to Ofsted operated mainly in the areas of lowest income (Vevers, 2008). Thus, although many settings were surviving the downturn successfully and there was an unexpected increase in demand for places for babies (Gaunt, 2009), the situation of the most disadvantaged and of those providing them with early childhood services was clearly deteriorating.

The impact on providers

In the summer of 2008 Thomson identified three ways in which the childcare sector was changing:

- The workforce was becoming better qualified.
- The total number of places was rising.
- However, more providers were facing immediate threats to their sustainability.

The picture was, therefore, a mixed one. It was possible, perhaps, to take comfort in the evidence that a reduction in quantity had been matched by improvements in quality. Ofsted's annual report for 2008/9 pointed to a doubling in the number of 'outstanding' judgements they had made (Ofsted, 2009a). It was clear from other evidence that the full story was more complicated. The private sector was pulling out of the Neighbourhood Nurseries Initiative. Major provider networks, which had begun to launch settings of their own in various places, were revising their expansion plans or even closing or selling the settings they already had. The decision by Nord Anglia to abandon the nursery sector (where it had once held a leading position) demonstrated that large commercial chains were not necessarily the answer to sustainability and quality. The collapse of the giant Australian nursery company ABC just as it was beginning to edge its way into the British market was an even more threatening indication of this. Worse was to come.

Figures issued by Ofsted early in 2009 appeared to show that the number of providers of all types was still falling (Ofsted, 2009b). The accuracy of these figures was queried by the PLA and other bodies and at the end of the year Ofsted issued data revised in the light of critical comment. However, Ofsted's quarterly figures (including those published a few days before the general election) showed a continuing drop in the number of places from that point onwards. Any economic crisis impacts differently on different parts of the population. There were still areas (by and large the most affluent) where provision was remaining steady in scale as well as improving in quality, but the picture was far from rosy. In this situation it was not surprising that there was renewed interest in care by nannies or close relatives.

The revival of 'informal' care

Nannies offered an obvious solution to those parents whose jobs paid well but forced them to require the kind of flexibility that registered day care settings or even childminders might find difficult to supply. The annual survey of nannies' salaries conducted by *Nursery World* showed a steep improvement in their pay in 2007. This raised again the question of how far they should be regulated. In 2005 a 'light touch' form of control had been introduced for nannies and other types of childcare provider not covered by Part Xa of the Children Act. This was updated in 2007. However, by the end of that year only 5 to 7 per cent of the nannies had registered. (In the absence of compulsory registration the total number of nannies can only be an informed guess.) There were financial advantages (in the form of tax breaks and childcare vouchers) for parents who employed people on the Voluntary Childcare Register, but at least some of them could afford to dispense with such assistance and there was little in the system for nannies themselves. The argument as to whether nannies or at least their agencies should be more tightly regulated had been going on for some time and looked set to continue.

The other type of informal care that started to attract renewed interest was care by grandparents (usually grandmothers). This had always been a more popular form of care for lower income families because it was cheap and did not entail contact with professionals who might be distrusted. More middle-class families had made less use of it, partly because of the tendency of upwardly mobile young adults to live in different parts of the country to their parents and partly because they were better disposed towards the profession-alism of registered settings. However, this began to change. A website called Grannynet was set up by a mother and daughter in the South East of England to foster mutual support among grandmothers. Another organization called Grandparents Plus campaigned for state subsidies for childcare provided by grandparents. They published the results of an opinion survey that indicated that some 60 per cent of people would support such a measure (Grandparents Plus, 2009) and lobbied Parliament. Together with the Equality and Human Rights Commission they published research demonstrating that many grand-parents faced hardship as a result of leaving or not entering paid employment in order to provide regular care for their grandchildren (Griggs, 2010). They argued that justice demanded that grandparents receive financial recompense for the support they were giving. Those who were more committed to tradi-tional family structures saw care by grandparents as a way of strengthening inter-generational relationships and providing pre-school children with less institutionalized forms of care.

Initial responses from the government and the early years professions were unenthusiastic. Research by Hansen and Hawkes (2009) suggested that children who attended nurseries had fewer behavioural problems and adapted more readily to the structured environment they found when they started school than children who had received regular care from grandparents. On the other hand, children who had been looked after regularly by grandparents appeared to be more articulate and it could be asked whether the structured environment of the average school was really suitable for a 5-year-old. A more impressive piece of evidence came from the example of the Netherlands. In 2005 that country had passed a childcare law that, among many other meas-ures, allowed grandparents to join the ranks of formal childcarers eligible for state subsidies. The consequences were problematic and took the Dutch government by surprise. It proved impossible to ensure the quality of the care given. At the same time the costs to government rose rapidly. By the end of

2009 the government in the Netherlands was planning to insist on qualifications or at least certain types of experience from grandparents who wanted to register as childcare providers and to lower allowances from the beginning of 2010. This example from abroad was not widely known here and there was strong support in England for a policy of subsidizing care by grandparents. The Conservative Party certainly found the idea attractive.

The consequences of devolution

By the time that Brown became prime minister the process of devolving political power from Westminster to new assemblies in Scotland, Wales and Northern Ireland was well established. As was said earlier in this book, there was a period when developments in other parts of the United Kingdom were noted in England because (on such matters as the appointment of Children's Commissioners) they seemed to offer models of better practice. By 2007 this was less clearly the case. England had followed the lead of the other nations, although with some modifications. (For example, the English Commissioner has fewer powers than the others.)

Developments in Scotland

A few weeks before Brown became prime minister the Scottish National Party (SNP) became the largest single party in the Scottish Parliament and was able to form a government there. They regarded early childhood as a priority. Their approach was in some respects very similar to that of the rest of the UK. Perhaps the most important way in which SNP policy was different was in the emphasis it put on devolution of power within Scotland – something that was partly a matter of principle, partly a matter of having to cope with the limitations imposed on them by having no overall majority in parliament. What the Scottish Government had to say about its partnership with local authorities had some similarities to the Westminster Government's approach to Local Area Agreements with local authorities in England. The SNP took things further, basing a lot of their work in this respect on a 'Concordat' with the Convention of Scottish Local Authorities. This built on earlier achievements in Scotland where local early childhood partnerships already appeared to be working more effectively than the EYDCPs in England and where ideas on workforce development were well in advance of those in England at the time (Children in Scotland, 2008).

Some consequences of the SNP's approach became clear quite early. For example, early in 2008 they decided not to roll out a programme of free nursery education for 2-year-olds that had been piloted in three local authorities, even though the evaluation team at Strathclyde University had not had the opportunity to report on their work. They justified this on the grounds that it was better to leave the decision on roll out to individual local authorities. Similarly, in July 2008 the Scottish Government withdrew advice that had been offered previously on the arrangements that local authorities should make with providers under Scotland's nursery grant scheme. The clearest indication of where they wanted to go came with the *Early Years Framework* in March of that year (Scottish Government and COSLA, 2008). This outlined aspirations similar to those in *Every Child Matters*, but did so in a way that emphasized more firmly the involvement of all partners at local and national level. The Scottish Framework and the new legislation on Children's Trusts in England are both too recent for systematic comparisons on their outcomes to be feasible, but it is clear that comparisons will continue to be made and may be helpful in determining which approaches are more effective.

Developments in Wales

In Wales attention was more focused on the early years curriculum, something that reflected the emphasis the Welsh Assembly Government wished to give to education in general. Soon after Brown became prime minister in London, Jane Hutt, the Minister for Education in Wales, issued the draft text for a new curriculum for children aged 3–7. As with the English EYFS there were critics who believed that this was still too focused on expected outcomes. The major differences were that the Welsh curriculum significantly modified the decisions made in 1870 that the fifth birthday should provide a crucial boundary, that the process of consultation, evaluation, training and implementation seemed to be more carefully considered, that the Welsh curriculum paid greater attention to issues of cultural diversity, and that (as in other aspects of education policy in Wales) a particular place was given to the promotion of the Welsh language.

The plan was that the new curriculum should be in operation for all children aged 3–7 years by the beginning of the school year 2011/12.

The desire to have continuity of planning was also illustrated by the decision to make the funding of Sure Start children's centres integral to 'Cymorth', a funding system catering for all children and young people. This was similar to what happened with Children's Trusts in England. The use of the phrase 'targeted support within the framework of universal provision' in the official documents might suggest some hazy thinking about the issue of whether services should be developed on a universal basis or be more explicitly focused on the disadvantaged, something that had also bedevilled work with children and young people in England.

Developments in Northern Ireland

In Northern Ireland the importance of developing early childhood provision from the poor base it had had in 1997 was one of several issues on which Sinn Fein and the Democratic Unionist Party found it possible to agree; so much so that cooperation with the Irish Republic on matters such as vetting people planning to work with children and the development of specialist services for young children with disabilities went ahead without arousing serious fears among Unionists. The steady progress that was being made in Northern Ireland was overshadowed by the cantankerous argument about the devolution of policing powers, which was not settled until 2010, but that progress did continue. In particular, the launch of the new Education and Skills Authority in 2008 laid the basis for better regulation of services.

The General Election of 2010

When Brown became prime minister he knew he had three years at most before a general election. In the event he kept going until almost the last possible moment. The election did not take place until 6 May 2010.

Disputes about early childhood services had played little part in the elections of 2001 and 2005. Differences between the parties seemed minimal, more a matter of the Conservatives being slightly less enthusiastic than anything else. The election of 2010 was inevitably dominated by the question of how to respond to the economic difficulties although other issues, especially immigration, probably influenced the outcome. Early childhood services were not much discussed. To some extent this was a reflection of the way society had changed. Few commented on the fact that the leaders of all three major parties were married to women who had both young children and successful careers of their own. This went unnoticed because it hardly seemed remarkable. Twenty-five years earlier it would have been surprising. Fifty years earlier it would have caused outrage. Now it was normal. In spite of this there were serious differences between the parties.

Ed Balls attempted several times during the election campaign to highlight the government's initiatives on early childhood services – so much so that at one time those who handled the Peppa Pig brand (which had been used in association with Children's Centres) seem to have become nervous that their children's cartoon character might become drawn into the political conflict in a partisan manner. The efforts that Balls made achieved little. Even if the economy and a vague desire for change had not dominated the election debates, it is doubtful whether many journalists would have been interested.

VOICES FROM THE TIME

The election campaign

Parents often tell me their local Sure Start is as important to them now as their local school – a great service open to all, a friendly place that offers support, advice and childcare that help the whole family. For Sure Start isn't only for the under-5s and their mums as some people think – more and more centres are welcoming dads, brothers and sisters and grandparents too. And it's not just the children and families who directly use Sure Start who gain from them; the neighbourhoods where they have opened are benefiting too. In many areas the children's centre is becoming a focal point for voluntary groups and other local services, helping to foster a stronger community spirit . . . Focusing Sure Start just on the poorest families would be a big step backwards. It is also divisive: there should be no place for this kind of segregated approach today. Like the NHS, Sure Start must be available for all.

Source: Ed Balls (16 March 2010). Taken from
http://www.edballs.co.uk (accessed 18 May 2010).

Sure Start children's centres have our full commitment because they set out the foundations for family support in every community. Now the centres are built, Labour thinks the job is done. They are wrong. The National Audit Office, Audit Commission and OFSTED have all criticised the Government's failure to develop Sure Start in a way that supports the poorest and most vulnerable families in our communities. Our plans and vision for Sure Start will change that. We will strengthen Sure Start for every family. Putting in place an extra 4,200 Sure Start Health Visitors – a new universal health visitor service, working through Sure Start to give every family access to the professional support they need in those critical early years.

Source: Maria Miller (17 March, 2010). Taken from
http://blog.conservatives.com (accessed 18 May 2010).

I am a Children's Centre Worker . . . My local area has a laughable shortage of health visitors. However, what I must ask is: are all these apparent new health visitors going to run play and stay sessions? deliver parenting programs? do outreach work? make home safety scheme assessments? staff contact sessions? arrange fun days? work evenings and weekends? signpost to adult education courses? Chase up any benefit and housing issues? And facilitate groups? All on top of the usual

Health Visitor job role? I accept there is a dire need for more health visitors but are they the Conservatives' only answer to Sure Start?

Source: Sam Walker (20 April 2010). Taken from http://blog.conservatives.com (accessed 18 May 2010).

When the election was over the Conservatives had more MPs than any other party, but not enough to give them a majority in the Commons. They went into coalition with the Liberal Democrats. Early childhood services had not featured much in the election campaign, but it had been clear from statements made on both sides that the Conservative approach now differed significantly from that of Labour. The implications of the coalition with the Liberal Democrats were less clear. The two parties shared some policies in this area – both, for example, had called for further revision of the Foundation Stage. In the past the Liberal Democrats had been more supportive of the idea of promoting additional services than the Conservatives. On the other hand, in the period before the election Annette Brooke, their principal spokesperson on children, had concentrated on issues such as safeguarding and disabilities rather than early childhood services. It was not clear whether this reflected her personal interests or the considered priorities of her party.

The first decisions made by the coalition government about early childhood were, inevitably, about ministerial appointments rather than policies. However, those decisions had clear implications for the future.

- The Department for Children, Schools and Families became the Education Department, although work with children's services remained part of the remit. This implied an intention to give greater attention to schools than early childhood services.
- The new Minister of State for Children and Families was a Liberal Democrat, Sarah Teather. Her professional background was in health and she had been her party's principal spokesperson on housing before the election. In other words, she did not have a particular track record on early years.
- Her Parliamentary Secretary was the Conservative MP, Tim Loughton. He had played a part in the development of his party's policies on children and young people, but his principal interest had been in issues concerning teenagers.
- Maria Miller, who had been the Conservatives' shadow minister for children and had carefully cultivated relations with organizations in early childhood services, was appointed to be a junior minister in Work and Pensions. Rumour had it that she would be focusing on life/

work balance. This would connect with earlier Liberal Democrat proposals to extend maternity and paternity leave.

The implications of these changes were that early childhood services would not be the priority for the new government that it had been for the one it replaced. Events before the election confirmed this. David Willetts, who had special responsibility in the Conservative Party for policy on the family, spoke of 'cooling it a bit' on Sure Start at a meeting organized by the Family and Parenting Institute (Morton, 2009). These comments produced a sufficiently hostile reaction to force him to back away for a while, but at a conference organized by 4Children in February 2010 he returned to the theme – claiming that 'excessive weight' had been placed on early childhood by the Labour government and that his party, once in power, would redress the balance (Faux, 2010).

One of the implications of the Conservatives' expressed desire to 'cool it' on Sure Start was that they seemed to be backing away, not just from new investment, but from the tentative moves already made towards integration of early childhood services. Although it was never stated clearly, the party appeared to favour the idea of day care for the youngest children when their parents wanted it and education for children aged 3 or 4. It was also indicative that one of the earliest cuts they made was in the budget of the Children's Workforce Development Council, whose principal task had been closer integration of professions concerned with children.

Comments made by Maria Miller in 2008 implied that her party might dispense with the new EYFS completely. She denied this and said she was anxious to avoid disruptive change (Gordon-Smith, 2009). It was difficult to make sense of the Conservative line on the EYFS. The curriculum guidance was a long way from being universally popular and a case for re-examining it could have been made. On the other hand, the idea of producing yet another version of the guidance so soon after the recent implementation would be an obvious example of Whitehall confusing the people delivering front-line services by bombarding them with new initiatives – something the Conservatives had frequently accused Labour of doing.

Altogether it was difficult to discern a coherent approach to early childhood services in things the Conservative Party had to say, but a general approach was clearly indicated. Different representatives of the party on different occasions spoke of a need to do the following:

- secure an early start to literacy and numeracy, something that might imply the introduction of more formal teaching methods at a fairly early age;
- increase the number of health visitors in order to provide support to first time mothers especially, something that suggested a stronger

focus on support within the individual family rather than in groups initiated and sustained by children's centres;

- give more support to childminders and to grandparents acting as regular providers of day care, something that implied a preference to childcare on domestic premises over childcare in nurseries or out-of-school clubs;
- make life easier in ways that were not clearly specified for private and voluntary providers;
- encourage the development of apprenticeships in childcare;
- focus the work of Sure Start on the most dysfunctional and disadvantaged families and pay staff partly on the basis of the results they achieved with such people.

In addition, the Conservatives identified Sure Start children's centres as being one of the types of public service they thought might be better run by staff cooperatives. Their proposals on cooperatives probably came from a desire to counter objections that they wanted to make it possible for big business to make big profits out of public services. By the time of the election they had done little to clarify how they saw such cooperatives being set up and operating. Similar ideas have worked well in some areas of public policy abroad. For example, in several parts of Spain staff cooperatives have played a significant and positive role in community psychiatric services. It was quite unclear in the period immediately after the election how far the coalition would develop this idea and whether children's centre cooperatives would be stand-alone local projects (perhaps a bit like the old Family Service Units) rather than the organizational basis for inter-agency coordination.

Some in the early years sector appeared to welcome things being said by the Conservatives before the election took place. In December 2009 *Nursery World* conducted a poll of practitioners to assess their views on political parties. While this demonstrated that people working in early childhood were as confused and disillusioned as the rest of the electorate, the Conservative Party had more support than any other (Defries, 2010a). It was difficult to discern how far this reflected approval of the party's stance on issues specific to the sector. It is possible that many of those who declared support for the Conservatives worked in the independent sector and anticipated that the party would treat them more favourably. In 2009 Miller had made friendly overtures to the Day Nursery Policy Group, a newly formed rival to the National Day Nurseries Association (NDNA) launched by providers disenchanted with the difficulties in many local authority areas over the administration of funding.

The specific proposals made by the Conservative Party did appear to be informed by a broad perspective, one with which Liberal Democrats might be expected to have some sympathy. Cameron was wary of returning to the sporadic attempts to push traditional moral values by the Thatcher and Major governments. He planned to take things a little distance in that direction, but not very far. In the interests of forming the coalition he was ready to ditch the token gesture his party had intended to make on giving married couples a small tax advantage.

By the time the coalition government had taken shape it was clear that the attempt by the previous government to give early childhood services at least a higher profile had failed. A revolution that falters is likely to go into reverse and this – to a large extent – is what appeared to be happening to the transformation of early childhood services the Labour Party had attempted since 1997.

Exercise

In the couple of years or so before the election David Cameron frequently spoke of the United Kingdom as being a 'broken society'. Not many people seemed to notice that precisely the same phrase was employed by Tony Blair in his 1996 book (p. 68) to describe the country after a long period of Conservative rule.

Like any piece of political rhetoric (especially one that both main political parties have used) talk of a 'broken society' is worth subjecting to critical examination.

- If society is now broken, when precisely was it not yet broken?
- When does a collection of specific social problems amount to a 'breaking' of society?
- If society gets 'broken' at any stage, to what extent can this be ascribed to the government of the day?
- How useful an analytical tool is the phrase?

Cameron cited the Doncaster case, where two children could easily have killed another child, as symptomatic of a much wider disintegration of society. Blair did the same nearly twenty years previously with the Bulger case. It is worth reading Loach's book *The Devil's Children* (2009) for her account of how earlier generations did not allow their horror at fatal attacks by some children on others to determine the severity of the response to the children involved or to draw wide-ranging conclusions about their society.

Further reading

In time books will become available on the 2010 election and its outcome. Publications dealing with the consequences for early childhood services will follow later. In the meanwhile the most obvious further reading to recommend would be the election manifestos of the various political parties.

8 Analysing the development of early childhood services under Labour

This chapter offers an assessment of the development of early childhood services in the period of the Labour government, 1997–2010. In particular it attempts to answer the following questions:

- How much changed in that period?
- To what extent were the changes that did take place due to the government?
- How solid were the foundations the government laid down for the continuing development of early childhood services?

Introduction

The Blair and Brown governments gave the issue of early childhood services much greater prominence. It is possible to have different opinions about the policies adopted, but there can be little doubt about the increased importance of this area of social policy. The question is whether the higher profile of the issue led to substantial change.

How much has changed?

The judgements people make about the scale of the changes that took place are governed by the expectations with which they started in 1997. Those who campaigned over a long period of time for a radical extension and restructuring of early childhood services see a situation that falls so far short of their objectives that they often argue little has changed. For others it is the contrast with the situation in the 1970s or earlier that is striking.

Some degree of change is evident. Perhaps I can give an example from my personal experience. In the mid-1970s I set up the first community play-scheme in Sheffield (where previously summer play activities had been organized by teachers on behalf of the local authority). I also organized a short training course for the local volunteers who ran the scheme. It is probably better for my self-esteem that the details of that course are now lost. At the time I had a limited understanding of what was required and there was not much guidance on the matter available. On the other hand, I did appreciate the potential of holiday playcare organized by parents who were supported by offers of training and resources. I now chair the management committee of an agency that supports playwork in a variety of ways, including courses leading to relevant qualifications. I am constantly impressed by the commitment of both our staff and the groups with which they work and the level of professional skill involved. In that respect, at least, the scale of change since the tentative efforts people like me were making in the 1970s seems obvious.

There are all sorts of ways in which the quality of the work being undertaken in early childhood settings is massively superior now to what was happening in the comparatively recent past. A few more examples can be cited:

- the quality of work with children under 3 and the developing appreciation of how much more they need than to be kept safe from physical harm;
- increased sophistication in the use of outside space for learning, something that was well understood in the 1920s and 1930s, but had largely been forgotten by the 1990s;
- the more or less universal adoption of key worker systems in day care;
- advances in specific areas of understanding that now inform practice. An example would be Athey's pedagogical development of Piaget's concept of 'schema' (Athey, 1990);
- the greater commitment to the principle of inclusion and the appreciation that this applies to several areas besides that of disabilities;
- openness to cultural diversity;
- increasing use of IT in both support to children's learning and improved communications between agencies;
- the influence of new ideas from abroad, for example the response to information about practice in Reggio Emilia;
- momentous increases in the scientific understanding of cognitive development and consciousness.

There have also been changes in the legal and administrative background:

- There have been important developments in qualifications and training, such as the Early Childhood Studies degree courses, the creation of Early Years Professional Status and opportunities for people working in either pre-school care or playwork to undertake training that will make transfer between the two areas of practice easier. Along with all that there has been work on the development of a proper framework for qualifications.

- A new system of regulation was devised for England in 2001. This produced a change in regulation criteria from one based almost exclusively on inputs to one based largely on outcomes, closer attention to what settings were doing about learning and emotional development as well as physical safety and the integration of the system of inspection for care and education.

- The changes that have taken place in the system of safeguarding are designed for all children, but have naturally had an impact on early childhood services. There are problems with the new system, but it does open up the possibility of greater clarity on the question of who should be permitted to work with children than the pre-1997 system of police checks and regulations governing who was to be considered disqualified. The fact that safeguarding is now located firmly in the context of support to parents has been especially important. There is a considerable contrast with the situation in the early 1990s when social services departments largely abandoned 'preventive' work with families to concentrate exclusively on child protection.

- Considerable work has gone into writing and implementing curriculum guidance for work with young children. Not everyone is happy with the results, but the question of the kind of approaches that are required is firmly on the agenda.

- Local authorities in England have new responsibilities for both supporting providers and for ensuring that provision is available. The commitment to this area of endeavour is much more extensive and carefully considered than it was under the pre-2001 permissive powers.

- Structures that have been created to promote partnership between different types of organization involved in early childhood services became an important feature of the plans those organizations make and the ways in which they are put into operation.

- Readily available statistical data have made judgements about what is happening in the early childhood sector much better informed.

- There is now a wider range of types of provision.

- Workers in nurseries and childminders are now more likely to possess qualifications and to benefit from the educational experience behind them.

- There are now more ways in which parents can receive financial help with access to early childhood services and new funding arrangements have been developed for some of the settings in more disadvantaged areas. The intention behind all this has been to make childcare more affordable. The evidence on whether they have been successful in this is mixed.

- The creation of the Sure Start Unit, the integration of inspection regimes within Ofsted and other measures are beginning to close the institutional gap between care and education, a gap that now has far fewer defenders than it did in the early 1970s.
- Children's centres are delivering new services that were not there before and have created structural opportunities for improved communication and cooperation between professionals from different agencies on a relatively local level.

So far I have spoken about changes specific to England. There have been comparable developments in Scotland, Wales and Northern Ireland. The freedom the other main parts of the United Kingdom now have to determine their own early childhood policies has created opportunities for experiment and probably acted as a driver for change.

What did not change

All this is significantly different from what existed before. However, change is complicated and not a matter of simple linear progression. Advances open up new issues that may create the need to reconsider what has been achieved. An example may illustrate what I mean. In the past it was often important to persuade those running playschemes or providing lunchtime supervision in primary schools that more was needed than keeping an eye on the children to ensure their safety. As this lesson was learned, the adults sometimes took over and organized the children's play in ways that undermined them and were potentially damaging for that reason. It then became necessary to persuade people to allow children to make their own decisions while providing the kind of environment that would facilitate their creativity and cooperation. This is a familiar pattern of development.

A key issue here is that there is still no settled public opinion as to whether childcare is good for children or not or whether it should be provided or subsidized by the state or not. Similarly, there is little agreement among the wider public on the sort of education that should be provided for young children. All attempts at change take place against this background and this is why politicians of all parties are often timid about the scale of change. This has an impact on developments in relation to the quality of practice.

There is still considerable reluctance outside the early years profession to accept the kind of understanding of child development that is common among practitioners. This explains some of the tensions between professional staff on the one hand and parents and politicians on the other.

Training has developed in many directions and there are new opportunities that were not there before. It can, however, be questioned how far we have moved beyond what was achieved by the old National Nursery Examination Board in the basic training of nursery nurses. In particular, the proposal made in 2009 by the Workforce Development Council to reduce the time available for basic courses in childcare and education poses the threat of a backwards move and one that seems to have been noticed by the union for college teaching staff (UCU) rather more quickly than by early childhood professionals.

Pioneers from Froebel to Piaget have an established place in the thinking of the early childhood professions. Those professions have not really caught up with recent advances in neuropsychology or even laboratory observation of young children. The findings of the relevant scientists are cited occasionally in polemics because they support points of view that had already been adopted. There is still far too little real recognition of the importance of scientific psychology for pedagogical practice.

We continue to be influenced by ideas from Europe (and occasionally from other 'developed' countries, such as New Zealand and the United States). We make little use of ideas from elsewhere. Practitioners have become sensitive to the fact that people from Africa, Asia or Latin America may follow different practices in relation to childcare and to the fact that these must be taken into account when working with children from those societies. There have been few attempts so far to question whether they have lessons for work with all children – whether that is about fairly practical matters, such as the best way to carry a baby, or questions about values, such as the responsibility of those in a community outside the nuclear family for a child's welfare.

Too many settings are in old, large buildings that were not intended for their current purpose when first built or in unimaginatively designed new premises. The issue of design and of how both the premises used by settings and the wider environment can better meet the needs of children has barely been raised. In part, of course, this is a matter of cost. It also stems from failure of imagination.

The value of books to young children is widely accepted and we have moved away from the snobbish attitude to picture story books critics displayed fifty years ago. Bookstart has made a modest but valuable contribution to this. At the same time there are still many practitioners who have a limited understanding of the opportunities that ICT offers for supporting children's learning. It also seems to be the case that few practitioners, apart from childminders who have more opportunities as they work in their own homes, have grasped how much good work has been undertaken by some of those producing TV programmes for very young children or considered how that material can be used.

There are important ways in which policies on early childhood and the administrative arrangements to support them have changed less than might have been expected.

The integration of care and education could have gone much further. In particular, the fact that funding streams for childcare and early education remain separate is a major psychological and practical stumbling block to coherent development.

The work of many community health personnel is still only loosely connected with that of other early years professionals. Cooperation still depends significantly on the personal relationships established by people who work together at neighbourhood level. In that respect, things have barely moved forward since the time of the NHS restructuring in 1974, which fractured the links that existed before then. This issue has become particularly important with the coalition government's identification of the health visiting service as an aspect of early childhood services to which they wish to give more emphasis.

We have yet to dispose of the idea that childcare, especially when associated with other forms of support offered to parents, is something the state should offer only to families on low income or that are considered in some way dysfunctional. Things are not as bad as they were in many social services department day nursery services in the 1960s and 1970s, but the problem is likely to become more salient as restrictions on public spending force the government to select priorities.

Partnership arrangements have barely begun to influence the way agencies operate. On the whole they have just provided another chore for middle managers to undertake. The structures put in place by the Labour government allow for more exchange of information than existed before and for greater clarity on what agencies can expect of each other. No one could object to that, but it is not a fundamental change. Where there is the will to move beyond the mere sharing of information, this can be inhibited by central government's expectations that its own priorities will prevail. In England neither of the two major parties appears ready to allow local authorities greater autonomy (although the situation is different in other parts of the UK). This reluctance to allow different places to do things differently often meets with approval outside the political sphere since it is easy to arouse hostility to any 'postcode lottery'. The insistence on consistency across the country is only compatible with the most limited kind of local initiative. In addition the independent sectors have not managed to establish positions of real influence within the bodies making plans for young children. 'Partnership' sounds nice – a cosy compromise between the ruthless market and the faceless bureaucracy of state-run provision. The reality is fine as far as it goes, but it does not go very far and it consumes a lot of administrative effort in the process.

Early childhood services are still too expensive for many families to make effective use of them. A large number do not even consider the option of regulated childcare. The fact that services are not affordable for many on low incomes does not arise from anyone making massive profits out of such services. Even the larger chains have had difficulties in making a financial success of things. To a worrying extent providers find it difficult to make enough money to be sustainable while their staff remain poorly paid for what they do.

This situation can only become worse as a significant number of families become poorer. When the number of settings first began to fall, there were some reasons not to feel alarm. Some of the decline was due to settings providing more than one service. Some of it was due to providers that could not meet new requirements going out of business, leaving – one might hope – higher quality provision to take their place. However, by 2010 the number of places was declining seriously.

There is some ambiguity about the advances made in safeguarding. The focus has been too narrowly on administrative measures rather than on the improvement of professional practice. The weakness of this is becoming apparent and should encourage a more critical view of Laming's proposals than is common among journalists or social workers. The case of Khyra Ishaq who died at home while supposedly receiving her education there demonstrated the limits of organizational change. The simple fact that the child's school, the home education service and the social workers were in the same local authority department did not by itself ensure effective cooperation between them. Above all, there is still too little concentration of effort on the business of communicating with children at risk. Within the safeguarding system they are often treated as more or less inert, though valuable, objects (at least until they become potentially stroppy teenagers). At one time local authority childcare inspectors were commonly accused of doing nothing at inspection but count the toilets. The allegation was unwarranted in many cases, but there was enough truth in it to suggest the need for reform. Now attention has turned largely from protecting children against accidental harm to protecting them from malice or neglect. The danger is that counting the assessment forms will replace counting the toilets. In both instances the problem is not the objective, but the way in which the concern to unearth one type of evidence (counting what can easily be counted) threatens to override getting to grips with the experience of the child herself. This is one significant respect in which regulation could have moved forward more substantially.

The role of the Labour Party and the contribution of other factors

The limits to the transformation that occurred are obvious. It is also worth asking how many of the changes that occurred were due to government action.

The answer to this question might seem obvious. The Labour Party were in power and they made the decisions that led to change. Like any political party happy with something they have done, they certainly wanted to take the credit for it. At the same time the pace at which change happened was determined at least as much by fear of what the press would say as it was by the desire to reform. The inept decision made in 2001 that childminders in England should be allowed to smack children and smoke in their presence as long as their parents consented demonstrated that the government was more afraid of the disapproval of the *Daily Mail* than they were of the response of the child-minders themselves, who were angry at being treated as second-class providers, people of whom less professional commitment and ability could be expected. Fear of the media also informed the even more important issue of direct provision by the state. In 1997 it seemed obvious to Blunkett that it was simply impossible for the state to provide universal childcare, although this is precisely what was happening in some other countries.

The desire of the Labour Party to reform early childhood services in 1997 was one of the things that led to improvements. Other factors were just as important.

The principal determining factor was what was happening in society without anyone planning it. More women with young children wanted to be in paid employment. More parents with ambitions for their children valued what early education might do for them. There were those who disapproved of these changes and probably many mothers suffered some degree of ambivalence about returning to work when their children were still young. Nevertheless, the trend was there. It revealed itself in the phenomenal development of the play-group movement, in the growth in the number of registered childminders in the 1970s and 1980s, in the development of community-based playcare towards the end of the 1980s and in the expansion of private nursery provision. If no government had done anything to encourage the growth of early childhood services, the demand for services would not have vanished. Perhaps the pace would have been slower and developments might have taken a different form. Some expansion would still have taken place.

The early years professions responded to all this. When Plowden's call for more nursery education fell victim to the gathering economic storm of the 1970s, early years specialists in the teaching profession responded by looking at ways of improving practice in those settings they already had. When the NNEB came in for heavy criticism in the late 1970s, some of those teaching future nursery nurses attempted to re-think the opportunities open to their students and encourage them to broaden their horizons. Universities and other research institutes developed new ideas on the ways in which early childhood services might be run. Several years before 1997 early years practitioners were beginning to discover a new self-confidence. The evolution of quality in practice relied more on that than it did on any initiatives the Labour government took.

Even in terms of action by government, things did not start from scratch in 1997. The Conservative governments of Thatcher and Major were responsible for some key reforms. The 1989 Children Act placed the welfare of the child at the heart of action by the state. The system of regulating childminding and day care introduced by that Act was considerably better than the previous one. The first attempt to define goals for early learning was another significant step forward. The extent to which it was radical is demonstrated by the inability of most TV journalists who bothered to report the matter to avoid sniggering at the very idea of an early years curriculum and by some of the criticism in the tabloid press. In many ways the reforms initiated during Blair's first period in office were a continuation of what the Conservatives had done.

In other words, the development of early childhood services between 1997 and 2010 was not the product of government policy alone. What the politicians did may have been critically important, but their actions were as much the result as the cause of any growth that did take place.

The solidity of the foundations

The success of any revolution is to be measured by the extent to which the changes it introduces survive the fall of the political leaders responsible for them. The National Health Service is a good example of that happening. Politicians, managers, health care staff and patients have often disagreed fiercely among themselves and with each other about the way the service should be organized. In spite of that, the institution remains so popular that no one has seriously suggested abandoning it since it was formed. No one could say that anything like that has been achieved for early childhood services.

It can be argued that the transformation does have some solid foundations.

The social changes that have generated demands for more and better and more affordable childcare and early education seem likely to continue, even if there are reverses. That process provides what is probably the most secure part of the foundation.

Improved understanding of what is possible and of the inextricable connections between care and education in the early years also has a chance of survival. The experience of the 1950s, 1960s and 1970s proves that understanding of the potential of those services may wither when social conditions do not sustain them. It also demonstrates that such gains never disappear entirely.

On the other hand, there are several ways in which the foundations are very weak.

Nowhere in the United Kingdom has a universal system of early childhood services been established. We have instead a patchwork of provision that can be confusing for parents and inadequate to meet all needs. The mix of funding streams bewilders everyone and wastes administrative resources. Attempts to remedy this in England by Brown's government met serious difficulties. An even more important fact is that there is little stomach anywhere in the political system for challenging the daft decision of 1870 to treat the fifth birthday as a crucial boundary point for education, even though the original motive behind that decisions (that politicians wanted young people to get out to work as soon as possible) has disintegrated with frequent changes in the school-leaving age since then.

Politicians of all parties recoil from the idea of a universal, government-led, free system of early childhood services, seeing it as too expensive to be considered. This needs more critical attention. When politicians say that something is not affordable, they really mean that they intend to spend money on something else instead. Those choices might be reasonable, but by saying that something cannot be afforded, rather than that it is something to which they wish to give a low priority, they suggest that the question of priorities is beyond debate. That is simply dishonest.

Whether the government could have driven through a universal system of service provision in the first decade of the twenty-first century, is open to doubt, given what is known about the state of public opinion on the matter. It remains the case that no real transformation was possible without a strategy of that kind.

The campaign of the Women's Liberation Movement in the 1970s to secure a universal childcare service was sometimes conducted in ways that were counterproductive. The movement had an aggressive style that reflected a wish to cast aside the expectations that women would be timid in asking for what they wanted. As a result they were sometimes careless about the way the demand for childcare was articulated, seemingly happy to give ammunition to their enemies who claimed that they were prepared to sacrifice the interests of children to those of selfish mothers. What was good about what they did is that it was precisely a campaign, focused on mobilization of those for whom the issue was important and launching community-controlled childcare projects to demonstrate what was possible and gather further support. In the course of the following decades the demand for better early childhood services took the form of lobbying rather than campaigning. Several developments were pivotal to this:

- In the 1970s the idea proposed by NUPE that childminders should be unionized was not well received by minders themselves and gave way to the idea of an organization that would promote good standards in childminding – NCMA.
- In the 1980s the National Child Care Campaign virtually wrote itself out of the picture when it launched the Day Care Trust as a body whose less obviously political activities would be able to attract new kinds of funding.
- In the late 1990s the introduction of the minimum wage forced pre-school playgroups to abandon the widespread practice of giving parents working at sessions on a rota basis fairly small sums of money

for this and thus hastened the trend towards pre-schools that were run by paid staff and in some ways were less under the direction of parents than the early PPA groups had been.

There were good reasons for these steps to have been taken. They contributed, however, to a situation where the effort that went into presenting solid research evidence to politicians became much more important than securing public support. Parents became consumers of services rather than the kind of participants they had been in some of the campaigning organizations of an earlier period. This left the expression of public opinion largely to journalists who did not necessarily have any stake in what was happening and were free to express sentiments that rested on older notions of what family life and childhood entailed rather than a sympathetic understanding of changes in society.

Lobbying by professionals often produces changes in the short term that do not survive because the public do not understand or like them. Throughout the second half of the twentieth century there were examples of professionals trying to secure reforms simply on the basis of their expert opinion rather than on the basis of public support. Sometimes they have taken politicians along with them by persuading them that any failure on their part to follow their advice would show them up as reactionary and unintelligent. Sometimes they have not. It has been all too rare for experts to engage in proper critical exchange with the politicians, let alone invest in persuading and informing the general public or listening to what they had to say. When they have been successful in getting the politicians to back them, they have been smug. When they have not, they have been sulky. The history of town planning and architecture after the Second World War provides an outstanding example. The experts never considered that those who did not like tower blocks and other innovations were worth time spent on them. As a result we ended up with urban structures that were inefficient, damaging to the environment, undermining of local enterprise and dangerous for children. There is every reason to be afraid that much the same sort of thing could happen in the field of early childhood services if the experts were more successful than they have been in lobbying the politicians.

A VOICE FROM THE TIME

Blaming the politicians for what has gone wrong

The suggestion that it is the ignorance of politicians that is the main obstacle to progress in early childhood services did not arise for the first time at the beginning of the current century, as the following brief passage makes clear:

[I]t is to be hoped that the future development of Nursery Schools and of infant education will not be frustrated by reactionary politicians, ignorant of the history of the subject and of the follies of their predecessors.

Source: (Rusk, 1933: 185)

Conclusion

The answer to the question 'Has there been a transformation in early childhood services?' cannot be 'Yes' or 'No' without qualification. Different aspects of what happened between 1997 and 2010 will suggest different answers. Clearly, we have not enjoyed steady progress from the situation that existed before 1997 towards some kind of ideal. Rather we have had a series of advances that have been undermined by unwillingness in government to consider truly radical solutions. It may have been a good idea to look beyond the two alternatives of free market competition or universal provision by the state. The model that was adopted has done too little to make early childhood services more attractive or affordable to many people. This situation can only get worse when we are facing severe economic difficulties and have a government that seems even more out of tune with the relevant professions than the one that ran things from 1997 to 2010. As a society we remain fundamentally uncertain where to draw the boundaries and lines of connection between the family, the community and the state when it comes to the welfare of young children. If those who speak for the early years profession think they have the answers, not many people are listening.

9 Evaluating recent developments in early childhood services

Introduction

The last chapter was concerned with the extent of the transformation of early years services under the Labour governments of 1997–2010. It asked how much had changed, how far that change was due to government initiatives and how much to other factors and, most crucially of all, whether the new arrangements had a solid foundation. It was about what happened as opposed to what should have happened.

It is especially problematic in the case of early childhood services to distinguish between technical issues, on the one hand, and moral or political issues, on the other. There are some fields in which the distinction is made more easily. The question of whether a bridge of a certain design will remain standing once it is in use is essentially a technical one. The question of whether the bridge should be built at all is a political one, associated with other questions about connections between communities, economic development, priorities in expenditure, and so on. The distinction is reasonably clear. When practitioners speak about the ways in which early years services should be organized, they bring expert professional knowledge to the discussion, but they cannot advocate policies on technical grounds alone. This is because children are also human beings. What we think should happen to them may reflect expert knowledge about, for example, the process of cognitive development, but inevitably it also reflects what we think it means to be a human being.

I do not intend to spell out here what I think of the changes since 1997 or what I would like to happen next. You may be able to make an intelligent guess from what has been said so far. The point of this chapter is to assist you to make up your own mind rather than persuade you that my personal opinions are worth adopting. Chapters 1–7 each ended with an exercise. This chapter is a set of exercises. I have outlined a set of questions inviting you to evaluate the situation we had reached by the spring of 2010. In each case a broad question is followed by a number of subsidiary ones. You may want to reflect on any or all of them on your own. You may see them as the basis for discussion with groups of colleagues. In all cases you can add to the specific questions two further ones:

- What are the implications of the judgements at which you have arrived for the future development of early years policy?
- Which of the political parties with any real chance of being in government comes closest to matching your perspectives (at least in relation to early years services)?

The questions are formulated in ways that address an English audience. If you are working in another part of the United Kingdom, you will need to reformulate them to make them relevant to your circumstances. However, the essential issues will remain the same whether you are looking at the answers proposed by the government in London, Edinburgh, Cardiff or Belfast.

The implication of the National Childcare Strategy was that a large number of children should receive care outside the family from an early age. Is this something you support?

- Is there any age (at least as an approximate guideline) below which you think care outside the family should be avoided?
- Even if you think there is a period in the life of most young children during which they should not receive care outside the family, are there circumstances where you would see this as better than the alternatives?
- In making these judgements how far are you taking for granted the ways in which society is organized at present? If you have reservations about the provision of day care to children below a certain age, do these reservations rest on nothing more than the kind of arrangements that are possible at present? Can you imagine a society so different (in terms of gender roles, flexibility of arrangements for paid employment, notions of wider responsibility for the welfare of children, etc.) that assumptions about the place of childcare would also have to be different?

Has the government helped to create a situation where the best forms of day care are readily available?

- Obviously, some settings are better than others. Do you also believe that some *forms* of day care are better than others for young children?
- Would you prefer to see pre-school children who spend part of the day being cared for by people other than their parents receiving that care in nurseries and other day care settings?

- Alternatively, would you prefer to see care provided inside the family home (by nannies) or provided by members of the wider family (such as grandparents) or by childminders?
- Whatever you think about these issues, do you think the government has done enough to make such options easier to access?

The latest version of the Foundation Stage Guidance modifies the previous guidance by extending the Phase backwards to birth and by altering in a minor way the boundary between pre-school and compulsory education. Do you approve of this change and would you like to see it taken further in the future?

- What do you understand by 'formal' education and how does it differ from other ways of supporting children's learning?
- Do you think the fifth birthday is an appropriate (if approximate) point at which compulsory education should begin or would you prefer some other birthday?
- How much flexibility should be exercised in the application of any such age boundary? If a degree of flexibility is permitted, who should make the decision to modify the usual rule about the start of compulsory education?

The government now offers support to parents in seeking day care outside the family and it was the policy of the Labour Party to encourage parents to make use of such services, especially where this meant families coming off benefit and into paid employment. Do you approve of this in general (whatever you think of the specific arrangements that have been made)?

- Should the state support all parents who want it with access to day care (by information services, subsidies or other means)?
- Should the state not only support parents who want day care for their children, but take steps to encourage parents to use such services as a way of reducing the number of families dependent on welfare benefits?
- Alternatively, should the state only facilitate or provide day care for parents who face problems they could not otherwise manage (including long-term sickness, poverty or family dysfunction)?

Current arrangements entail a variety of subsidies to parents (nursery education grants, tax credits, childcare vouchers) as well as direct subsidies to some providers in areas of significant deprivation, but leave parents having to meet some of the costs. Do you

approve of this general approach (even if you think there are problems with existing arrangements that require resolution)?

- Should all such services be free at the point of access as they are in some other countries?
- Alternatively, should services be paid for by those parents that want them (with, perhaps, the possibility of those responsible for the safeguarding of children paying for such services in certain limited circumstances)?
- Should neither of those extreme options apply, but all parents be asked to contribute to costs according to their income and general needs as the price they pay for greater freedom in choosing the services they will use?

The Labour government attempted to achieve a balance between two objectives – making services affordable and accessible for all parents and securing variety in the services available, partly to offer parents more choice. Whether or not you think they have been successful in seeking such a balance, were they right to attempt it?

- How important is the availability of different services to the development of innovative ideas on day care and early education?
- How much importance do you ascribe to parents being able to select the type of service they want or to choose to make use of none of them?
- Is it so important that early years services should be affordable and easily accessible that it is worth sacrificing parental choice to ensure this can happen?

Diversity in provision is a matter, not just of types of setting, but also of the nature of providers. In order to facilitate parental choice and to keep down the costs to the taxpayer, the government has encouraged provision by commercial organizations and by voluntary or community-based agencies. Do you approve of this?

- Would you like to see the government do more to encourage particular forms of ownership of settings, such as more direct provision by local authorities, higher state subsidies to voluntary and community-based providers, similar help to childminders or measures to make it easier for commercially organized ventures to flourish? If you would like to see such measures taken, would this be to encourage greater diversity or to give one particular kind of provider a stronger role?

- If you want one type of provider to have the leading role, what is your reason for this?
- If you think diversity is a good thing in general, how important is it to have diversity within a fairly small area or is it just necessary to ensure a measure of diversity across the country?

The Labour government took forward the measures designed to foster inclusion that were initiated by the Conservatives in the period 1979–1997. In particular, it applied the SEN Code of Conduct to pre-school settings, widened the inclusion agenda and required providers to address cultural diversity in all settings, not just those receiving children from minority groups. How do you evaluate this change?

- Would you distinguish in any way between the various equality issues that have been raised?
- Do you share the Labour government's view that diversity and community cohesion are opposite sides of the same coin or do you believe that there are tensions between acceptance of variety, on the one hand, and cohesion on the other?
- How far has the inclusion agenda helped in the positive development of the curriculum for *all* children?

The decision to transfer responsibility for the regulation of day care and childminding from local authorities to Ofsted in England and to the Assembly Government in Wales was one of the first major changes made by Labour in the field of early childhood services. By the time of the 2010 election the government seemed to believe that this reform had had the desired effect and that there should be a smaller role for regulation in the provision of day care and home-based care. Do you agree with this shift in policy?

- How useful is regulation as a way of driving up standards (bearing in mind that many of the countries whose early childhood services are admired in this country have less regulation than we do)?
- Should regulation focus on preventing bad practice or on encouraging the development of better practice in all settings? (For an argument from the USA that it should concentrate on preventing bad practice, see Clarke-Stewart, 1991: 59.)
- Has it been a good thing that various inspection regimes have been brought under one organizational umbrella in England?
- How important is it that all such services are governed by the same principles? If you think it is important, do you believe that

bringing inspection regimes together in one organization is necessary to secure this?

For a long time there has been a growing consensus that the welfare of children is a paramount consideration, one that must be allowed in some circumstances to override the wishes of parents. This was clearly reflected in the move from the concept of parental rights to that of parental responsibility in the 1989 Children Act. Whatever mistakes people may have made in particular cases of child protection, do you believe that this approach is the right one?

- Do you think priority should be given to supporting parents to care for their children or to rescuing children at risk? If both are important in different circumstances, how do you distinguish between those circumstances?
- Even support to parents (as opposed to initiatives taken that separate children from their parents) involves intervention by agents of the state in family life. What is your view on the boundaries between the state and family and what are the implications of this for safeguarding?

Labour moved away from the situation in which early childhood services were left to parental choices, the mechanisms of the market and the interventions of those charged with safeguarding children. It wanted greater coordination at national, local authority and neighbourhood level. Do you see this as a positive move or one that threatens to undermine initiative and innovation?

- Do you think that enough has been done (in legislation and funding arrangements) to eradicate what many have seen as an artificial distinction between care and education in services for young children?
- Do you think coordination has to be directed by central government or can be left more to those operating at local authority level?
- Do we need greater coordination between community health services and care/education services for young children?
- Do you believe that coordination can only be effective if it happens at the most local level, leaving parents and professionals in a relatively small area free to determine their own priorities?

The Labour government had a developing strategy for universal early years services and made clear that it wanted to see at least one Sure Start children's centre in every local authority ward eventually. Do you think this was the right approach?

- Do you think the state should restrict what it does in this sphere to supporting those families and communities that appear to be failing their children?
- Alternatively, do you think that the Labour government did not go far enough and should have moved much more quickly towards a system of universal provision of highly coordinated services?

How do you evaluate what happened between 1997 and 2010?

- Do you think the Labour Party got their policy more or less right (even if it got some details wrong), moving forward in the right direction, at a pace that made it possible to build more effectively and reviewing each step as it was taken?
- Alternatively, do you think they made some serious strategic errors? If so, what do you think these were? Were they wrong to move towards universal access at all when the role of the state should be more restricted or do you think they should have adopted a model of universal, free provision similar to that in some other European countries?
- Where should we go from here? What should be the future of early childhood services across the United Kingdom?

This chapter has asked you to consider several issues. You might find it useful to read a brief article by Peter Moss published in 2010 just before the general election. In it, he suggests five things he would like to see happen next:

- the completion of a fully integrated system of early childhood education and care by 2025;
- giving all children access to children's centres;
- replacing market mechanisms in provision by democratic control and collaboration;
- reducing the drive to standardization and encouraging more experimentation in the type of services provided;
- creating a better relationship between early childhood services and the school system.

Does that model appeal to you? If not, why not? If it does, what steps do you think need to be taken by government in the immediate future and what do you think practitioners and those involved in their education and continuing support can do to achieve it?

10 Conclusion

The last two chapters moved from a relatively straightforward chronological account of what happened as early childhood services were developed in this country to analysis and evaluation of the 'transformation' attempted in the period 1997–2010.

Behind all the specific issues addressed in those two chapters there is one that is fundamental and provides the rationale for looking back over a fairly lengthy period of time rather than just the recent past. The process of moving from a predominantly rural society to a modern, urbanized one threw up many new questions about the way families should function and how they should relate to the wider society. Those questions cannot be answered once and for all, because the situation itself is still in flux. The fundamental question of what should be the relationship between individual families, the communities in which they find themselves and the state remains a problematic and contentious one and will do so for some time to come. Any plans we make for the development of early childhood services have to be provisional. The needs they are intended to meet will change over time. If better childhood services are provided, that will itself be one factor leading to greater change.

This is not a new dilemma. It is one that has informed the way we live for centuries. The question requires constant reformulation. It would be untrue to say we are moving forward in a simple direction towards a goal that can be described even if it is not yet attained. That is why if you read a book or pamphlet from the first half of the nineteenth century you may be surprised on one page to read something about the need to encourage the natural desire young children have to learn or the importance of observations that might (apart from the actual phrasing) have come from a modern text book and yet a few pages further on be equally surprised to find the author warmly recommending a particularly graphic account of how God massacred the citizens of Sodom and Gomorah as ideal material for a young child just starting to learn how to read. It is also why we need to be alert to the failure of the society in which we currently live to get to grips with the fundamental issue effectively.

While I was working on this book, I learned from *Nursery World* about a series of incidents that have now been largely forgotten. At the time the Second World War was nearing its close and in the period immediately afterwards trains were frequently delayed for several hours. When mothers who had taken their babies on long train journeys wanted to breastfeed they were frequently too embarrassed to raise this with other passengers in overcrowded carriages and put off feeding as a result. Their children could become seriously dehydrated. At least two appear to have died. In 1946 the Derbyshire Women's Institute led a campaign to demand the provision of special coaches for nursing mothers. The train companies prevaricated, having their hands full with the proposed nationalization of the railways. Nothing came of the campaign.

I have been involved with many cases of child abuse, but I found these stories distressing in a quite different way. The fact that no one had intended any harm somehow made the suffering and waste that took place seem even worse. Of course, we do not need to revive the campaign of the Derbyshire WI. Such things could not happen now. Long train journeys are usually faster. Facilities on the trains themselves and in stations are much better. The alternative of car travel is more readily available. The materials for artificial feeding are much improved. Travel companies and local authorities often declare themselves to be 'breastfeeding friendly' – a slightly clumsy phrase, but a welcome development. What happened in 1945 and 1946 is almost certain not to be repeated. In spite of that, the fundamental situation that led to those incidents is still with us in a variety of ways. The mothers felt unable to explain their dilemma to the other passengers. Those people noticed nothing was amiss or were too embarrassed to mention it. The railway companies and the state were reluctant to organize things differently, probably feeling that it was up to mothers whether or not they undertook such journeys. No one was certain what to expect of anyone else. The particular problem might not be repeated, but it would be easy to identify similar uncertainties about the respective roles and obligations of parents, other people and the state today. The most optimistic assessment of the transformation since 1997 would have to recognize the many difficulties for parents that still exist, the unresolved conflicts of opinion about what should happen and the disadvantages to children that result. Until those issues are addressed more sensitively and intelligently, any major developments in early childhood services are bound to have a shaky foundation.

Timeline 1811–2010

This timeline is designed to help you relate developments in the history of early childhood services in the UK with each other and with other historical events. The second column is concerned with political, social and cultural history. The third column lists Acts of Parliament, official reports, etc. relating to early childhood services. The fourth column lists initiatives by individuals or organizations, including key publications.

Year	Historical events	State initiatives and interventions	Independent initiatives and key publications
1811		Inquiry into education in London	
1812	Anti-machine disturbances		
1813			Owen's *A New View of Society*
1814			New Lanark School opens
1815	Battle of Waterloo		
1816			Lancaster splits from his own Society
1817	Death of Jane Austen		
1818		Inquiry into education outside London	
1819	Repressive measures against unrest		
1820			Wilderspin opens Spitalfields School
1821	First steam ferry across Channel		
1822	Death of the poet Shelley		
1823	Large-scale penal reforms		
1824	Trade unions legalized		Infant School Society formed
1825	Stockton to Darlington Railway opens		
1826			Froebel's *The Education of Man*

Continued

Year	Historical events	State initiatives and interventions	Independent initiatives and key publications
1827			Glasgow Infant School Society
1828			Wilderspin visits Scotland
1829	Metropolitan Police Force formed		Wilderspin begins spread of infant schools in England
1830	Manchester and Liverpool Railway		
1831	Brunel's design for Clifton Bridge		
1832	Great Reform Act		
1833		First government grants to schools	
1834	Poor Law Amendment Act		
1835	Municipal Corporations Act		Fox Brothers' workplace creche
1836	Laws against child employment		Hill's National Education
1837	Registration of births, etc.		
1838	First Presentation of Charter		
1839		Committee on Education formed	
1840	Modern postal system starts		Wilderspin's System of Infant Education
1841	First full census		Chartist Statement on Education
1842	Second presentation of Charter		
1843	Euston Station opens	Extension of schools grants system	
1844	Reform of law on banking		
1845	First road to have tarmac		Wilderspin opens his last school
1846		Teacher-Pupil Scheme	
1847	First medical use of anaesthetics		
1848	Third presentation of Charter		
1849			Froebelian Women's College in Berlin opens
1850			Day nurseries open in several towns
1851	Great Exhibition in London		
1852	Great Ormond Street Hospital		Bill to set up local authority schools systems

1853	Saltaire model industrial town		
1854	Charge of the Light Brigade		Grants for teacher training
1855			Books on Kindergarten system published here
1856	Bessemer steel process		
1857	India taken over by government		First Kindergarten outside London
1858			
1859	Darwin's *Origin of Species*		
1860		Infant schools praised by Commission	Kindergarten in Leeds
1861	First tram in London		Ladies Sanitary Reform Association
1862	Speed of light measured	Payment by results system	Barlee's *Visit to Lancashire*
1863	Football Association launched		
1864	Clifton Bridge completed		
1865	First woman doctor qualifies		Survey of working mothers in Manchester
1866	Trans-Atlantic cable in use		
1867	Second Reform Act		*Lancet* calls for day nursery in every parish
1868	Inquest condemns babyfarmer		
1869		Education Act	Greenwood's *Seven Curses of London*
1870	Franco-Prussian War	New Schools Code	
1871	Bank holidays invented	Infant Life Protection Act operational	
1872			
1873			Bland's first MoH Report
1874			MoH in Bolton calls for nurseries in every parish
1875	Public Health Act		
1876		School attendance compulsory	
1877	Electric light invented		
1878	Microphone invented		

Continued

Year	Historical events	State initiatives and interventions	Independent initiatives and key publications
1879			Froebel Society launches teacher training college
1880			
1881		Payment by results ended	
1882	Married Women's Property Act		
1883			NSPCC formed
1884	Third Reform Act		
1885	Invention of motor car		
1886		Cross Commission	
1887	Riots in London		
1888	County Councils established		National Froebel Union
1889	Prevention of Cruelty to Children Act		NSPCC founded
1890			First use of term 'nursery school'
1891		School fees abolished	
1892			Norland Institute opened
1893		Circular 322 approves Froebel	
1894			Froebel Education Institute opens
1895			Sully's book on child development
1896	First modern Olympics		
1897		Female Sub-Inspectors of Schools	
1898	First electric railway opens		
1899		National Board of Education formed	
1900	Labour Party launched		
1901	Death of Queen Victoria		
1902	Radioactivity discovered	Education Act	
1903	Cow & Gate baby milk		McMillan moves to London
1904	Report on 'Physical Deterioration'		
1905		Report on Under-5s in Schools	

1906		Free school meals	National Society of Day Nurseries formed
1907	Model T Ford car	Schools Medical Service	
1908	Bakelite (first plastic) produced		
1909	Constitutional crisis		
1910	Power of Lords reduced		
1911			McMillan's Open Air Camp in Deptford
1912			*The Montessori Method*
1913			Child Welfare Conference in London
1914	First World War starts	Care of Mothers and Young Children Act	
1915			
1916	Battle of the Somme		
1917	Communist Revolution in Russia		First nursery class (Manchester)
1918	End of War		
1919	Lady Astor first woman MP		
1920	Ministry of Health formed		
1921	Irish Free State formed		
1922	Cuts in public expenditure		Nursery Schools Association formed
1923	Reorganization of railways		Isaacs opens Malting School in Cambridge
1924	First Labour Government		
1925			
1926		Reductions in nursery education grants	
1927	First talking movie		Westminster Health Society starts nursery
1928	All women over 21 get vote		Montessori International Association
1929	Wall Street Crash		
1930	Birdseye market frozen peas		
1931	White Paper on expenditure cuts		First exams for nursery nurses
1932			
1933		Hadow Report on nursery education	

Continued

Year	Historical events	State initiatives and interventions	Independent initiatives and key publications
1934		Milk in Schools Act	
1935	Driving test introduced		Nursery Nurses Association
1936		Circular 1444 on nursery education	
1937	999 calls invented		Association of Children's Librarians formed
1938	Midwives Act		
1939	Start of Second World War		
1940	Many evacuated children return home		
1941		Registered Daily Guardians Scheme	
1942	Beveridge Report		
1943			Mothercraft Training Centre opens
1944	Education Act		
1945		Family Allowances introduced	NNEB formed
1946		Local authorities responsible for day care	
1947	International Monetary Fund	Nurseries and Childminders Regulation Act	
1948	Children's Departments set up		
1949	First jet airliner built		
1950	Contraceptive pill invented		
1951	Conservatives win election		
1952			Clydesdale Road Adventure Playground
1953			Playground Committee of NPFA
1954	End of food rationing		
1955			Local authorities run nursery nursing exams
1956			Review of nursery nursing syllabus
1957	EEC (start of European Union)		
1958	Race riots in London		Spock's Baby and Child Care published in UK

1959	Russian spaceship on moon		
1960		Halt to new nursery schools	PPA formed
1961	Commonwealth Immigration Act		
1962			
1963		Children and Young Persons Act	
1964	Labour win election	Nursery places for teachers	
1965		Inquiry on childminding	
1966			
1967		Plowden Report	
1968	Start of Women's Liberation	Revision of law on regulation	
1969	Conservatives win election		
1970			
1971			
1972	World oil crisis	Social services departments	
1973		Education: A Framework for Expansion	Jacksons' research project on childminding starts
			Nursery Action Group formed
1974		Children Act	
1975		Sunningdale Conference	
1976			
1977			NCMA formed
1978		Circular on coordinating services	
1979	Conservatives win election		
1980			National Childcare Campaign
1981			Brierley Report on NNEB
1982			National Out of School Alliance (later 4Children)
1983		Workplace nursery benefits taxed	Pen Green opens
1984			Workplace Nurseries Campaign
1985			Labour Party Charter for Under-5s

Continued

Year	Historical events	State initiatives and interventions	Independent initiatives and key publications
1986		Clark Report on early education	Day Care Trust formed
1987			
1988	National Curriculum		
1989		Children Act	
1990		Rumbold Report	
1991		DoH guidelines on regulation	
1992		Implementation of Part X (Children Act)	
1993		Circular 93/1 on over-rigid regulation	
1994			CACHE formed
1995			PPA becomes PLA
1996		*Desirable Outcomes*	
1997	Labour win general election		
1998		*National Childcare Strategy*	
1999		Protection of Children Act	
2000		*Foundation Stage Guidance*	
2001		Transfer of regulation to Ofsted	
2002		*Birth to Three Matters*	
2003		*Every Child Matters*	
2004		Children Act	
2005		Children's Commissioner for England	
2006		Childcare Act	
2007		DCSF established	
2008		New Foundation Stage in force	
2009		Apprentices, Skills, Children and Learning Act	
2010	Coalition government		

Bibliography

Abbott, L. (2002) *Birth to Three Matters: A Framework to Support Children in their Earliest Years*. London: DfES.

Abbott, M. (2003) *Family Affairs: A History of the Family in Twentieth Century England*. London: Routledge.

Abel-Smith, B. and Townsend, P. (1965) *The Poor and the Poorest: A New Analysis of the Ministry of Labour's Family Expenditure Surveys of 1953–54 and 1960*. London: G. Bell & Sons.

Allen of Hartwood, Lady (1946) Why not use bomb sites like this? *Picture Post*, 16/11/46, 26–7.

Ambler, M., Armstrong, D. and Hawksworth, J. (2003) *Universal Childcare Provision in the UK: Towards a Cost-benefit Analysis*. London: PriceWaterhouseCoopers.

Anning, A. and Edwards, A. (eds) (1999) *Promoting Children's Learning from Birth to Five: Developing the Early Years Professional*. Buckingham: Open University Press.

Athey, C. (1990) *Extending Thought in Young Children: A Parent-teacher Partnership*. London: Paul Chapman.

Baldock, P. (2001) *Regulating Early Years Services*. London: David Fulton.

Baldock, P., Fitzgerald, D. and Kay, J. (2009) *Understanding Early Years Policy*, 2nd edn. London: Sage.

Barlee, E. (1863) *A Visit to Lancashire in December 1862*. London: Seeley & Co.

Beeton, I. (1861) *Beeton's Book of Household Management*. London: S.O. Beeton.

Belsky, J., Vandell, D., Burchinall, M., et al. (2007) Are there long-term effects of early childcare? *Child Development*, 78: 681–701.

Benjamin, J. (1974) *Grounds for Play*. London: National Council for Social Service.

Best, J. (1962) Baby sitters, *Nursery World*, 63(1882): 11.

Beveridge, W. (1942) *Social Insurance and Allied Services: Report Presented to Parliament by Command of His Majesty*. London: HMSO.

Biddulph, S. (2006) *Raising Babies: Should Under-3s Go to Nursery?* London: Harper Thorsons.

Bilton, H. (1998) *Outdoor Play in the Early Years: Management and Innovation*. London: David Fulton.

Black, J. (2001) *The Making of Modern Britain: The Age of Empire to the New Millenium*. Stroud: Sutton Publishing.

Blackstone, T. (1971) *A Fair Start: The Provision of Pre-School Education*. London: Allen Lane.

Blair, T. (1996) *New Britain: My Vision of a Young Country*. London: Fourth Estate Ltd.

Blunkett, D. (2006) *The Blunkett Tapes: My Life in the Bear Pit.* London: Bloomsbury.

Bond, J. (1989) Child care can mean big business, *Nursery World*, 27/7/89, 12–14.

Bone, M. (1977) *Pre-school Children and the Need for Day Care.* London: Office of Population, Censuses and Surveys.

Boulton, A. (2008) *Memories of the Blair Administration: Tony's Ten Years.* London: Simon & Schuster.

Bowlby, J.A. (1963) *Child Care and the Growth of Love.* London: Penguin.

Brehony, K.J. (1999) Among women: the participation of men in the Froebel and Montessori Societies. Paper presented to the History of Education Society's Annual Conference on 'Breaking boundaries: gender, politics and the experience of education', 5 December.

Brehony, K.J. (2000) The kindergarten in England 1851–1918, in R. Wollons (ed.). *Kindergartens and Cultures: The Global Diffusion of an Idea.* London: Yale University Press, 59–86.

Brice Heath, S. (1997) Child's play or finding the ephemera of home, in M. Hilton, M. Styles and V. Watson (eds) *Opening the Nursery Door: Reading, Writing and Childhood 1600–1900.* London: Routledge, 17–30.

Brierley Report (1981) *A Future for Nursery Nursing.* London: National Nursery Examination Board.

Briggs, F. (1978) The development of nursery nursing and the changing role of the nursery nurse (1870–1975). Unpublished MEd thesis, University of Sheffield.

Brown, H. (1998) *Unlearning Discrimination in the Early Years.* Nottingham: Trentham.

Bruner, J.S. (1966) *Studies in Cognitive Growth.* Cambridge, MA: Harvard University Press.

Bruner, J.S. (1980) *Under Five in Britain.* London: Grant McIntyre.

Bryant, B., Harris, M. and Newton, D. (1980) *Children and Minders.* London: Grant McIntyre.

Campbell, A. (2007) *The Blair Years: The Alastair Campbell Diaries.* London: Hutchinson.

Central Policy Review Staff (1978) *Services for Young Children with Working Mothers.* London: HMSO.

Chandiramani, R. (2010) Tories to abolish children's trust obligations if they win election, *Children and Young People Now*, April, 1.

Charmley, J. (2008) *A History of Conservative Politics Since 1830.* London: Palgrave Macmillan.

Charlton, V. (1977) A lesson in day care, in M. Mayo (ed.) *Women in the Community.* London: Routledge & Kegan Paul, 31–44.

Chesser, E.S. (1903) *Women, Marriage and Motherhood.* London: Cassell.

Children in Scotland (2008) *Working it Out: Developing the Children's Sector Workforce.* Edinburgh: Children in Scotland.

Clark, M.M. (1987) *Children Under Five: Educational Research and Evidence*. London: Gordon & Breach Science Publishers.

Clark, M.M. and Waller, T. (eds) (2007) *Early Childhood Education & Care: Policy and Practice*. London: Sage.

Clarke, P. (2004) *Hope and Glory: Britain 1900–2000*. London: Penguin Books.

Clarke-Stewart, A. (1991) Day care in the USA, in P. Moss and E. Melluish (eds) *Current Issues in Day Care for Young Children: Research and Policy Implications*. London: Department of Health in association with the Thomas Coram Foundation, 35–60.

Comenius, J.A. (1956) *The School of Infancy* (ed. E.M. Eller). Chapel Hill: University of North Carolina Press.

Community Relations Commission (1976) *Who Minds? A Study of Working Mothers and Childminding in Ethnic Minority Communities*. London: CRC.

Cross, C. (1969) Obesity in childhood, *Nursery World*, 69(2272): 10–11.

Crowe, B. (1983) *The Playgroup Movement*, 4th edn. London: Unwin.

Cusden, P. (1938) *The English Nursery School*. London: Kegan Paul.

David, T. (ed.) (1994) *Working Together for Young Children: Multi-professionalism in Action*. London: Routledge.

Day Care Trust (2009) Nursery fees continue to rise, but why? *Nursery World*, 29/1/09, 10–11.

Day Care Trust and National Centre for Social Research (2007) *Childcare Nation? Progress on Childcare Strategy and Priorities for the Future*. London: Day Care Trust.

Defries, M. (2010a) Sector warms to Tory election win, *Nursery World*, 7/1/10, 4.

Defries, M. (2010b) Mothers vote for staying at home, *Nursery World*, 18/2/10, 5.

De Giustino, D. (1975) *Conquest of the Mind: Phrenology and Victorian Social Thought*. London: Croom Helm.

De Lissa, L. (1939) *Life in the Nursery School*. London: Longmans, Green & Co.

Department for Children, Schools and Families (DCSF) (2007) *The Children's Plan: Building Brighter Futures*. London: DCSF.

Department for Children, Schools and Families (DCSF) (2009) *Next Steps for Early Learning and Childcare: Building on the Ten-Year Strategy*. London: DCSF.

Department for Children, Schools and Families (DCSF) & Department for Business, Innovation and Skills (2009) *Understanding Attitudes to Childcare and Childcare Language Among Low Income Parents*. London: DCSF.

Department for Education & Employment (DfEE) (1998) *Meeting the Childcare Challenge: A Framework and Consultation Document*. London: HMSO.

Department for Education and Employment (DfEE) and School Curriculum and Assessment Authority (SCAA) (1996) *Desirable Outcomes for Children's Learning on Entering Compulsory Education*. London: DfEE & SCAA.

Department for Education and Skills (DfES) (2001) *Schools: Achieving Success*. London: DES.

Department for Education and Skills (DfES) (2003) *Every Child Matters*. London: DES.

Department of Education and Science (DES) (1967) *Children and Their Primary Schools* (The Plowden Report). London: HMSO.

Department of Education and Science (DES) (1973) *Nursery Education* Circular 2/73. London: DES.

Department of Health (DoH) (1991) *The Children Act 1989: Guidance and Regulations, Volume 2 Family Support, Day Care and Educational Provision for Young Children*. London: HMSO.

Department of Health & Social Security (DHSS) and Department of Education and Science (DES) (1976a) *Low Cost Day Provision for the Under Fives*. London: HMSO.

Department of Health & Social Security (DHSS) and Department of Education and Science (DES) (1976b) *The Coordination of Services for All Children Under Five*. London: HMSO.

Department of Health & Social Security (DHSS) and Department of Education & Science (DES) (1977) *Combined Nursery Schools and Day Centres*. London: HMSO.

Dickens, C. (1865) *Our Mutual Friend*. London: Chapman & Hall. Re-published as a Penguin Classic in 1985 by Penguin Books (Harmondsworth).

Disraeli, B. (1845) *Sybil or The Two Nations*. Re-published in 2008 by Oxford University Press.

Dwork, D. (1987) *War is Good for Babies and Other Young Children: A History of the Infant and Child Welfare Movement in England 1898–1918*. London: Tavistock.

Dykins, M. (2008) Life in the PPA – looking back – looking forward, in Wales Pre-School Playgroup Association *Memories of the Playgroup Movement in Wales 1961–1987*. Cardiff: Wales PPA, 31–3.

Early Childhood Unit (1991) *Ensuring Standards in the Care of Young Children: Registering and Developing Quality Day Care*. London: National Children's Bureau.

Elfer, P. and Beasley, G. (1991) *Regulation of Childminding and Day Care: Using the Law to Raise Standards*. London: National Children's Bureau.

Elias, E. (1969) When East meets West, *Nursery World*, 6/6/69, 18–19.

Evans, M. (2003) Paying off? *Nursery World*, 13/11/03, 10–11.

Evans, M. (2009) Early years low priority for NHS, *Nursery World*, 26/3/09, 10–11.

Faux, K. (2010) 'Excessive weight' is placed on early years, says Tory MP, *Nursery World*, 4/3/10, 4.

Frankenberg, R. (1966) *Communities in Britain: Social Life in Town and Country*. London: Penguin Books.

Fynne, R.J. (1924) *Montessori and Her Inspirers*. London: Longmans, Green & Co.

Gallagher, A. (1977) Women and community work, in M. Mayo (ed.) *Women in the Community*. London: Routledge & Kegan Paul, 121–41.

Garland, C. and White, S. (1980) *Children and Day Nurseries: Management and Practice in Five London Day Nurseries*. London: Grant McIntyre.

Garwood, J. (1988) Working class mothers, child care and infant mortality in late nineteenth century Macclesfield: the problems involved in researching women's history. Unpublished dissertation for MA in Women's Studies, Sheffield Polytechnic.

Gaskell, E. (1848) *Mary Barton: A Tale of Manchester Life*. Re-published in 2008 by Vintage Books (London).

Gaunt, C. (2006a) Poverty levels fall in Sure Start areas, *Nursery World*, 3/8/06, 5.

Gaunt, C. (2006b) UK declared nation of deprived children, *Nursery World*, 10/8/06, 5.

Gaunt, C. (2009) Crunch drives babies into daycare, *Nursery World*, 12/3/09, 4.

Giles, J.E. (1852) *A Warning to British Parents and Citizens against State Education in General and the Manchester and Salford Local Scheme in Particular*. London: Charles Gilpin.

Goldschmied, E. and Jackson, S. (1994) *People Under Three: Young Children in Day Care*. London: Routledge.

Gopnik, A., Meltzoff, A. and Kuhl, P. (1999) *How Babies Think*. London: Orion.

Gordon, P., Aldrich, R. and Dean, D. (1991) *Education and Policy in England in the Twentieth Century*. London: Woburn Press.

Gordon-Smith, P. (2009) Time for the sector to talk to the Tories, *Nursery World*, 22/1/09, 16–17.

Grandparents Plus (2009) *Re-thinking Family Life: Exploring the Role of Grandparents and the Wider Family*. London: Grandparents Plus.

Greaves, J.P. (1827) *Letters on Early Education by J.H. Pestalozzi Addressed to J.P. Greaves Esq. Translated from the German Manuscript with a Memoir of Pestalozzi*. London: Sherwood, Gilbert & Piper.

Greenwood, J. (1869) *The Seven Curses of London*. London: Stanley Rivers and Co. Re-published in 1981 by Basil Blackwell (Oxford) with an introduction by Jeffrey Richards.

Griggs, J. (2010) *Protect, Support, Provide: Examining the Role Played by Grandparents at Risk of Poverty*. London: Grandparents Plus and Equality & Human Rights Commission.

Hadow, W.H. (1933) *Infant and Nursery Schools*. London: HMSO.

Hakin, C., Bradley, K., Price, E. and Mitchell, L. (2008) *Little Britons: Financing Childcare Choice*. London: Policy Exchange.

Halloran, H. (1982) The diverse role of the nursery nurse and its implications for future education and training. Unpublished MEd thesis, University of Manchester.

Hanley, M.P. (1981) Educational provision in Ancoats, Manchester, during the nineteenth century. Unpublished MEd thesis, University of Manchester.

Hansen, K. and Hawkes, D. (2009) Early childcare and child development, *Journal of Social Policy*, 38(2): 211–39.

Harrison, N. and Barnett, U. (1983) *The First 80 Years (1903–1983): A Short History of the Westminster Health Society/Westminster Children's Society*. London: Westminster Children's Society.

Harrison, T. (ed.) (1943) *War Factory: A Report by Mass Observation*. London: Gollanz.

HEDRA Consulting (2007) *What Is the Impact and Cost Implication of Extending the Free Early Education Entitlement? Final Report*. London: Department for Children, Schools and Families.

Hewitt, M. (1958) *Wives and Mothers in Victorian Industry: A Study of the Effects of the Employment of Married Women in Victorian Industry*. London: Rockliff.

Hill, F. (1836) *National Education: Its Present State and Prospects*. London: Charles Knight.

Hirsch, D. (2009) *Through Thick and Thin: Tackling Child Poverty in Hard Times*. London: Campaign to End Child Poverty.

Hobsbawm, E.J. (1969) *Industry and Empire*. London: Penguin Books.

Home Office (1998) *Supporting Families*. London: HMSO.

Horn, P. (1997) *The Victorian Town Child*. Stroud: Sutton Publishing.

Howe, L. (1814) *Hints for the Improvement of Early Education and Nursery Discipline*. London: J. Hatchard.

Hughes, M. (1942) Mothers and woman power in relation to nurseries, foster mothers and daily minders, *Mother and Child*, 13(5): 91–5.

Jackson, B. and Jackson, S. (1979) *Childminder: A Study in Action Research*. London: Routledge & Kegan Paul.

Jenkins, S. (2007) *Thatcher & Sons: A Revolution in Three Acts*, 2nd edn. London: Penguin Books.

Jones, L. (1924) *The Training of Teachers in England and Wales*. Oxford: Oxford University Press.

Joseph, Sir K. (1972) *Caring for People: An Attempt to Identify the Scale and Nature of Social Need*. London: Conservative Central Office.

Karmilov-Smith, A. (1992) *Beyond Modularity: A Developmental Perspective on Cognitive Science*. Cambridge, MA: MIT Press.

Keeble Hawson, H. (1968) *Sheffield: The Growth of a City 1893–1926*. Sheffield: J.W. Northend Ltd.

Knight, B. (1975) *Report of the First National Conference on Childminding*. Cambridge: National Educational Research and Development Trust.

Labour Party (1985) *A Charter for the Under-Fives*. London: Labour Party.

Laming, Lord W.H. (2003) *The Victoria Climbié Inquiry*. London: HMSO.

Lane, J. (1999) *Action for Racial Equality in the Early Years*. London: National Early Years Network.

Lawson, J. and Silver, H. (1973) *A Social History of Education in England*. London: Methuen.

Leissner, A, Herdman, K.A.M. and Davies, E.V. (1971) *Advice, Guidance and Assistance: A Study of Seven Family Advice Centres*. London: Longmans.

L'Estrange, R. (1686) *An Account of the General Nursery or Coledge of Infants, Set up by the Justices of the Peace for the County of Middlesex, with the Constitutions and Ends Thereof*. London: Roberts.

Lewis, J. (1984) *Women in England 1870–1950: Sexual Divisions and Social Change*. Brighton: Wheatsheaf Books.

Liddiard, M. (1924) *The Mothercraft Manual*. London: Churchill.

Loach, L. (2009) *The Devil's Children: A History of Childhood and Murder*. London: Icon Books.

Lovett, W. and Collins, J. (1841) *A New Organization of the People, Embracing a Plan for the Education and Improvement of the People*. Reprinted in 1969 by Leicester University Press.

McCann, P. and Young, F.A. (1982) *Samuel Wilderspin and the Infant School Movement*. Beckenham: Croom Helm.

Mackinder, J. (1925) *Individual Work in Nursery Schools*. London: London Educational Publishing Company.

Macmillan, H. (1938) *The Middle Way: A Study of the Problem of Economic and Social Progress in a Free and Democratic Society*. Wakefield: E.P. Publishing.

McMillan, M. (1930) *The Nursery School* (revised edition). London: J.M. Dent.

MacInnes, T., Kenway, P. and Parekh, A. (2009) *Monitoring Poverty and Social Exclusion: 2009*. London: Joseph Rowntree Foundation.

Makins, V. (1997) *Not Just a Nursery . . . Multi-agency Early Years Centres in Action*. London: National Children's Bureau.

Manchester Statistical Society (1834) *On the State of Education in Manchester*. Manchester: Manchester Statistical Society.

Marbeau, J-B, F. (1845) *Crèches pour les petits enfants d'ouvrières ou Moyen de diminuer la misère en augmentant la population*. Paris: Comptoir des imprimeurs-unis.

Mercer, A. (2002) Nursery schools win new Labour respect, *Nursery World*, 27/6/02, 9.

Mercer, M. (1996) *Schooling the Poorer Child: Elementary Education in Sheffield 1880–1902*. Sheffield: Sheffield Academic Press.

Ministry of Education (1945) *The Nation's Schools: Their Plan and Purpose*. London: HMSO.

Ministry of Health (1945) *Circular 221/45*. London: HMSO.

Minns, R. (1980) *Bombers and Mash: The Domestic Front 1939–1945*. London: Virago.

Montessori, M. (1912) *The Montessori Method: Scientific Pedagogy as Applied to Child Education in 'The Children's Houses'*, trans. A.E. George. London: Heinemann.

Moore, G. (1894) *Esther Waters*. Republished in Oxford World's Classics, edited by D. Skilton in 1983, Oxford: Oxford University Press.

Morton, K. (2009) 'Cool it' on early years, say Tories, *Nursery World*, 9/7/09, 4.

Moss, P. (2001) End of term report, *Nursery World*, 4/1/01, 10–13.

Moss, P. (2010) Early childhood education and care: five steps to better provision, *Nursery World*, 4/2/10, 12–13.

Mulcaster, R. (1581) *Positions: Wherein those Primitive Circumstances be Examined which are Necessarie for the Training up of Children Either for Skill in their Book or Health in their Bodie*. London: Thomas Vautrollier.

Nathan, C.H. (1943) Children's nurseries, *Nursery World*, 29/4/43, 401.

National Audit Office (2006) *Sure Start Children's Centres*. London: The Stationery Office.

National Centre for Social Research (2010) *Families Experiencing Multiple Disadvantage: Their Use of and Views on Childcare Provision*. London: Department for Children, Schools and Families.

National Children's Homes (2003) *United For Children? How Devolution is Impacting Upon Children*. London: NCH.

National Evaluation of Sure Start Research Team (2005) *Early Impact of Sure Start Local Programmes on Children and Families: NESS Report no.13*. London: DfES.

National Foundation for Educational Research (2003) *Towards the Development of Extended Schools*. Nottingham: DfES Publications.

National Union of Teachers (NUT) (1929) *The Education of Children up to the Age of Seven Plus*. London: NUT.

Newson, J. and Newson, E. (1965) *Patterns of Infant Care in an Urban Community*. Harmondsworth: Penguin Books.

Newson, J. and Newson, E. (1968) *Four Years Old in an Urban Community*. London: Allen & Unwin.

Nursery World (1925) The pioneer of nursery training colleges: a great Victorian. One woman's beliefs, *Nursery World*, 9/12/25, 59.

Nursery World (1943) Nursery life and family life, *Nursery World*, 15/7/43, 597.

Ofsted (2009a) *The Annual Report of Her Majesty's Chief Inspector of Education, Children's Services and Skills (2008/9)*. London: Ofsted.

Ofsted (2009b) *Registered Childcare Providers and Places in England*. London: Ofsted.

Osborn, A.F. and Milbank, J.E. (1989) *The Effects of Early Education: A Report from the Child Health and Education Study*. Oxford: Oxford University Press.

Owen, R. (1813) *A New View of Society: Essays on the Principles of the Formation of the Human Character and the Application of the Principle to Practice*, re-printed in Claeys, G. and Owen, R. (2007) *'A New View of Society' and Other Writings*, London: Penguin Classics.

Owen, S. (1989) The 'unobjectionable' service: a legislative history of childminding, *Children & Society*, 4: 367–82.

Owen, S. (2006) Organised systems of childminding in Britain: a sociological examination of changing social policies, a profession and the operation of a service. Unpublished dissertation for the University of California, Santa Cruz.

Palmer, S. (2006) *Toxic Childhood: How the Modern World is Damaging Our Children and What We Can Do About It*. London: Orion Books.

Paneth, M. (1944) *Branch Street: A Sociological Study*. London: Allen & Unwin.

Parrock, J. (1989) Child care at the factory gate, *Nursery World*, 9/2/89, 15.

Pascal, C. and Bertram, T. (2006) Second class?, *Nursery World*, 2/2/06, 10–11.

Pearson, G. (1975) *The Deviant Imagination: Psychiatry, Social Work and Social Change*. London: Macmillan Press.

Penn, H. (1997) *Comparing Nurseries: Staff and Children in Italy, Spain and the U.K.* London: Paul Chapman Publishing.

Penn, H. (2005) *Understanding Early Childhood: Issues and Controversies*. Maidenhead: Open University Press.

Perkin, J. (1993) *Victorian Women*. London: John Murray.

Pinchbeck, I. and Hewitt, M. (1969) *Children in English Society*, Volume One: *From Tudor Times to the Eighteenth Century*. London: Routledge & Kegan Paul.

Preyer, W. (1882) *Die Seele des Kindes*. Leipzig: Grieben. First translated into English by H.W. Brown in 1893 as *The Mind of the Child*, London: Longmans, Green & Co.

Prideaux, S. (2005) *Not So New Labour: A Sociological Critique of New Labour's Policy and Practice*. Bristol: The Policy Press.

Proud, J. (1810) *Six Discourses Delivered to Young Men and Women on the Most Interesting and Important Subjects of Life and Practice*. London: Eaton.

Pugh, G. (ed.) (1988) *Services for Under Fives: Developing a Coordinated Approach*. London: National Children's Bureau.

Pugh, M. (2008) *State and Society: A Social and Political History of Britain since 1870*, 3rd edition. London: Hodder & Stoughton.

Qualifications and Curriculum Authority (QCA) and Department for Education and Employment (DfEE) (2000) *Investing in Our Future: Curriculum Guidance for the Foundation Stage*. London: QCA and DfEE.

Rentoul, J. (2001) *Tony Blair: Prime Minister*. London: Little, Brown & Co.

Riley, D. (1983) *War in the Nursery: Theories of the Child and Mother*. London: Virago.

Ronge, B. (1855) *A Practical Guide to the English Kindergarten*. London: A.N. Myers.

Rose, J. (2006) *Independent Review of the Teaching of Early Reading*. London: DfES.

Rose, J. (2009) *Independent Review of the Primary Curriculum: Final Report*. London: DCSF.

Rumbold Report (1990) *Starting with Quality: Report of the Committee of Inquiry into the Educational Experiences Offered to Three and Five Year Olds*. London: Department of Education & Science.

Rusk, R. (1933) *A History of Infant Education*. London: University of London Press.

Russell, J. (1874) *Children Playing: Its Blessings and Lessons*. Sheffield: St. Philip's Church Sunday School.

Schools Curriculum and Assessment Authority (1996) *Desirable Outcomes for Children's Learning on Entering Compulsory Education*. London: HMSO.

Scottish Government and COSLA (2008) *The Early Years Framework*. Edinburgh: The Scottish Government.

Seebohm (1968) *Report of the Committee on Local Authority and Allied Personal Social Services*, Cmnd. 3703. London: HMSO.

Séguin, E. (1846) *Traitement moral, hygiène, et éducation des idiots et des autres enfants arriérés en retarde dans leur développement, agités de mouvements involuntaires, débiles, muets non-sourds, bégus etc.*, re-published in 1997 by Association pour l'étude de l'histoire de la sécurité social (Paris).

Séguin, E. (1847) *Jacob-Rodrigues Pereire . . . notice sur sa vie et ses travaux et analyse raisonnée de sa méthode*. Paris: J-B Baillère.

Séguin, E. (1866) *Idiocy and its Treatment by the Physiological Method*. New York: A.M. Kelley.

Seldon, A. (2004) *Blair*. London: Free Press.

Selleck, R.J.W. (1994) *James Kay-Shuttleworth: Journey of an Outsider*. London: Woburn Press.

Sheffield City Council (1992) *Corporate Childcare Strategy: Options for Change*. Sheffield: City Council.

Shinman, S. (1979) *Focus on Childminders: A Profile of the First Bunbury Drop-In Centres*. London: Inner London Pre-School Playgroup Association.

Siraj-Blatchford, I. (2000) *Supporting Identity, Diversity and Language in the Early Years*. Buckingham: Open University Press.

Sloane, R. (1989) Does the playgroup need updating?, *Nursery World*, 1/6/89, 20–1.

Spock, B. (1958) *Baby and Child Care*. London: The Bodley Head.

Stanniland, A. (1989) Women, work and childcare: a local history of childcare provision in Sheffield of the 1940s and 1950s. Dissertation submitted for the MA in Women's Studies at Sheffield Polytechnic.

Stanton, T. (ed.) (1884) *The Woman Question in Europe: A Series of Original Essays*, re-printed in 1970 by Source Book Press (New York).

Steedman, C. (1990) *Childhood, Culture and Class in Britain: Margaret McMillan 1860–1931*. London: Virago.

Strategy Unit (2002) *Delivering for Children and Families: Report of the Interdepartmental Childcare Review*. London: Cabinet Office.

Sully, J. (1895) *Studies of Childhood*. London: Longmans, Green & Co.

Sure Start Unit (2003) *Sure Start: Making Life Better for Children, Parents and Communities by Bringing Together Early Education, Childcare, Health and Family Support*. London: DfES.

Taylor, S.J.L., Lord and Chave, S. (1964) *Mental Health and Environment*. London: Longmans, Green & Co.

Tebbitt, N. (1991) *Unfinished Business*. London: Weidenfield & Nicholson.

Thompson, F.M.L. (1988) *The Rise of Respectable Society: A Social History of Victorian Britain 1830–1900*. London: Fontana Press.

Thomson, R. (2004) Change targets says Labour MP, *Nursery World*, 8/7/04, 5.

Thomson, R. (2008) The sector in numbers, *Nursery World*, 218/08, 13.

Tweed, J. (2002) Labour's early years job 'is not finished', *Nursery World*, 14/2/02, 4.

Urben, E. (1977) A case study of child-minders in the London Borough of Camden, in M. Mayo (ed.) *Women in the Community*. London: Routledge & Kegan Paul, 45–51.

Vevers, S. (2003) Taking advantage, *Nursery World*, 12/6/03, 10–11.

Vevers, S. (2005) Ten year strategy: ways and means, *Nursery World*, 6/1/05, 10–11.

Vevers, S. (2008) Quality of childcare: poorest provision is in deprived areas, *Nursery World*, 9/10/08, 10–11.

Vidal, F. (1987) Jean Piaget and the liberal Protestant tradition, in M.G. Ash and W.R. Woodward (eds) *Psychology in Twentieth-Century Thought and Society*. Cambridge: Cambridge University Press, 271–94.

Von Marenholtz-Bülow, B. (1855) *Woman's Educational Mission: Being an Explanation of Frederick Fröbel's System of Infant Gardens*, translated by Elizabeth, Countess Krockow von Wickerode. London: Darton & Co.

Watson, V. (1997) Jane Johnson: a very pretty story to tell children, in M. Hilton, M. Styles and V. Watson (eds) *Opening the Nursery Door: Reading, Writing and Childhood 1600–1900*. London: Routledge, 31–46.

Welshman, J. (2006) *Underclass: A History of the Excluded 1880–2000*. London: Hambledon Continuum.

Whalley, M. (2007) *Involving Parents in their Children's Learning*. London: Paul Chapman Publishing.

Wheeler, O.A. and Earl, I.G. (1939) *Nursery School Education and the Reorganisation of the Infant School*. London: University of London Press.

Whitbread, N. (1972) *The Evolution of the Nursery-Infant School: A History of Infant and Nursery Education in Britain 1600–1970*. London: Routledge & Kegan Paul.

Wilderspin, S. (1824) *The Importance of Educating the Infant Poor from the Age of Eighteen Months to Seven Years, Containing an Account of the Spitalfields Infant School and the New System of Instruction There Adopted*, 2nd edn, London: G. Goyder. Reprinted in 1993 by Routledge/Thoemmes Press.

Wilderspin, S. (1840) *A System for the Education of the Young Applied to All the Faculties Founded on Immense Experience on Many Thousands of Children in Most Parts of the Three Kingdoms*. London: James S. Hodson.

Willan, J. (2009) Revisiting Susan Isaacs – a modern educator for the twenty-first century, *International Journal of Early Years Education*, 17(2): 151–65.

Williamson, S. (1989) Child care at the workplace, *Nursery World*, 26/1/89, 14–15.

Wilson, E. (1977) *Women and the Welfare State*. London: Tavistock.

Wintour, P. (2006) Blair admits failing most needy children, *Guardian*, 16 May.

Women's Group on Public Welfare (1943) *Our Towns 1939–1942*. Oxford: Oxford University Press.

Wood, G. (1934) The history and development of nursery education in Manchester and Salford. Unpublished MEd. thesis, University of Manchester.

Woolley, H. (1670) *The Compleat Servant-maid or The Young Maiden's Tutor*. London: Thomas Passinger.

Wright, B. (1999) *A History of the National Nursery Examination Board*. St. Albans: Council for Awards in Children's Care and Education.

Wynne, R. (1936) Pre-school lessons: how to prepare your child for school, *Nursery World*, 21: 540, p.676.

Young, M. and Willmott, P. (1962) *Family and Kinship in East London*. Harmondsworth: Penguin Books.

Yudkin, S. and Holme, A. (1963) *Working Mothers and Their Children: A Study for the Council for Children's Welfare*. London: Michael Joseph.

Zeliger, V. (1985) *Pricing the Priceless Child: The Changing Social Value of Children*. New York: Basic Books.

Index